LOURDES - "THE HEART OF GOD'S MERCY":
Accounts and reflections of a pilgrim

LOURDES - "THE HEART OF GOD'S MERCY":
Accounts and reflections of a pilgrim

"God, whom I serve with my spirit in preaching the Gospel of his Son, is my witness..." <u>Romans 1 vs 9</u>

"Ndinodaro *nokuti Mwari iye wandinoshandira nomwoyo wangu wose nokuparidza kwandinoita Shoko (Dama) Rakanaka roMwanakomana wake, ndiye chapupu changu...*" <u>**Romans 1 vs 9**</u>

"In the Name of the Father, and of the Son and of the Holy Spirit. Amen."

HAIL MARY
"Hail Mary, full of grace. The Lord is with thee. Blessed art thou among women, and blessed is the fruit of thy womb, Jesus.
"Holy Mary, Mother of God, pray for us sinners, now and at the hour of our death. Amen."

Joseph Foroma

Copyright © 2021 Joseph Foroma.

LOURDES - "THE HEART OF GOD'S MERCY": *Accounts and reflections of a pilgrim*

ISBN: 978-1-77920-668-8

First Printed in 2021

Book design by Daniel Mutendi
Part of front cover background image by Elena Joland, unsplash.com

Front and back cover designs by Daniel Mutendi

<u>Cover photos:</u>
The photos of Our Lady and that of St Bernadette provided by and used with the kind permission of the Sanctuaire ND de Lourdes, Pôle Communication.

ACKNOWLEDGEMENTS

I am eternally indebted to my brother Mr Benjamin Takavarasha, who offered numerous Novenas and daily encouragement so that I would never give up on completing this work. This is a brother who gave me a shoulder to lean on whenever he read the body language, or noticed I was undergoing a setback of whatever nature. An ever present in my life. I often think that without his support this work may never have been completed.

My sincere appreciation to my local parish priest at Our Lady and St Joseph Catholic parish Fr Anthony Cho who has kindly provided the foreword to this book.

Posthumous acknowledgement note: Fr Paul Dynan
With the family's kind permission I record my deep appreciation, posthumously, to my late parish priest Fr Paul Dynan who had agreed to foreword this book on its completion and publication. Ever the pillar of support to me and my family in both our personal and parish lives, he was called to the heavenly home in 2020 before this work was completed. His successor parish priest Fr Anthony Cho very kindly agreed to fulfil the task his brother priest had undertaken to do and am very grateful to Fr Anthony for providing a beautiful foreword to this book.

Requiem aeternam dona eis, Domine. Et lux perpetua luceat eis.
Fidelium animae, per misericordiam Dei, requiescant in pace.
Amen.

FR PAUL DYNAN

Before her passing on to the Lord's heavenly home in 2009 I once asked my mother if she would be willing to go on pilgrimage with me. She told me that this would not be possible due to her advanced age (she was then in her 80's). And she added that if I would go on pilgrimages myself, Our Lady would be pleased and would acknowledge that I had also gone on her behalf. Over the years I have tried to keep that commitment to my late mother.

The book was massively enriched by a cross section of testimonies by pilgrims I met at Lourdes and some whom I travelled with on my various annual pilgrimages there. I came to realise that the genuine stories of these people of faith in telling the wonderful story of the mercy of God at Lourdes are priceless.

I have tried to take every care to present as accurate a narrative as possible and of course ultimately take full responsibility for any inaccuracies or errors.

As I wrote this book, I remembered too my many early mentors and school teachers who include: the late Sr Assumpta Ribeiro, the nursing midwife at my birth who received me from my mother's womb into the world at Gokomere Mission and who I was to meet regularly later as an adult in her next role in charge of the orphanage at Driefontein Mission. I was very close to this wonderful 'grandma' of mine. Such was her impact on me that if ever I was travelling anywhere near her Mission station I would always detour and see her even for only a few minutes, often for longer. The other icon in my life was the late Sr Ancilla Mahuni, my Year One class (Sub A as it was called then) teacher. On what was my final encounter with her on 5 and 6 January 2018, she flattered me in front of her other elderly Sisters at their Ugandan Martyrs retirement home saying I had never been any trouble to her in my first year in school! The others are Mr Richard Chinyuku who took me through my other early years 3 to 5 at Gamanya School at Chivhu. I remember too with respect and fond memories my secondary school teachers who include Mr Abdul Madubeko, the late Mr John Mupfumira, Mr late Engelbert Marume, the late Br Roger Martinueau, the late Br Clement, the late Mr Chirawu, the late Mr Cuthbert Musiwa, Mr Norman Maposa, Prof Francis Gudyanga, Fr Patrick Makaka SJ who presided over my wedding and became a lifelong friend, and others. Without their focussed and dedicated formation and efforts in my early life the gifts of faith, numeracy and literacy would not have come my way.

FOREWORD

During the past year, we have been deprived of travelling for pilgrimages and for leisure. In the Diocese of Brentwood, our annual summer pilgrimage to Our Lady's Shrine in Lourdes has also been cancelled twice. I have been helping as a Chaplain to the Handicapped Children's Pilgrimage Trust (HCPT) Groups since 2017, where we accompany young pilgrims from the Bishops' Conference of England and Wales during the Easter Octave week - these pilgrimages have also been suspended due to the global Coronavirus pandemic. I am very certain that this has affected many families and others.

This publication brings fond memories of pilgrims who have travelled far and wide with steadfast faith, asking our Blessed Mother's intercessions with great confidence and hope.

In the Homily of His Holiness Pope Benedict XVI on the occasion of the 150th Anniversary of the Apparitions of the Blessed Virgin May (dated 14th September 2008), Pope Emeritus Benedict XVI reminds us that the primary purpose of the Shrine at Lourdes, *"is to be a place of encounter with God in prayer and a place of service to our brothers and sisters, notably through the welcome given to the sick, the poor and all who suffer"*. © Copyright 2008 - Libreria Editrice Vaticana. (Used with permission). During this time of pandemic, where millions around the world have suffered so much through the sickness and death of family members and loved ones, I believe it is most fitting to seek Mary as Our Mother, given to us by Jesus himself; who is always receptive to the needs of her children where the Light of Christ streams from her face and God's mercy is made manifest.

Dependent on the intercessions of Our Lady; although we cannot be physically present at the Holy Shrine of Our Lady of Lourdes, we are able to be *spiritually* present through our fervent and persistent prayer. This book is a channel that can lead us on our continued journey of faith. As Pope Benedict rightly stated, "our lives so often shrouded in darkness, she [Mary] is a beacon of hope who enlightens us …"

For me this book is an inspiration, evoking many fond, happy and nostalgic memories of my pilgrimages to Lourdes. I congratulate Joseph Foroma on its successful completion and thank him for his conscientious sourcing of the contributions and testimonies of many pilgrims. To the pilgrims, I thank you for your generosity in sharing your profoundly personal reflections. This book is truly motivational and I look forward with great confidence to all of us pilgrims gathering again at Our Lady's Shrine in Lourdes.

May St Bernadette pray for us and Our Lady, who revealed herself as the Immaculate Conception, accompany all people of goodwill, all those who suffer in heart or body, to raise their eyes towards the Cross of Jesus, so as to discover there (in Lourdes) the source of life, the source of salvation.

Fr. Anthony Cho
Solemnity of the Ascension of the Lord
13th May 2021

"To one who has faith, no explanation is necessary. To one without faith, no explanation is possible." <u>St Thomas Aquinas</u>

DEDICATION

I dedicate this book to my late parents, and their parents Bernadette Soubirous lived a short life. She died aged only 35 years. But her short life and her encounters with Our Lady (the Blessed Virgin Mary) left a strong legacy and powerful messages worthy of many reflections. As was the case with Bernadette one does not need to live a long life to make significant and memorable differences to others. Indeed, the lives and impacts of many other Saints attest to this fact too. Touching the lives of others is a crucial way of spreading The Good News of Our Lord Jesus Christ. And this is what Bernadette did and continues to do to this day. Bernadette leads us to Our Lady, who as Fr Michael Gaitley of the Marian Fathers of the Immaculate Conception (MIC) says, Mary is *"the surest, easiest, shortest and most perfect means to becoming a saint."* Our Blessed Mother is therefore the best way to get to her son Our Lord Jesus Christ and therefore the Kingdom of heaven.

I went to Lourdes for the first time in 2014 and went every year since then until the coronavirus pandemic and so was unable to make the pilgrimage in 2020. I have written and hereby share my own reflections as well as the testimonies of others about this holy place. I devote some time to reflect on how some of the aspects of Bernadette's life could be applied to guide and shape our own Christian living. Bernadette was a mortal being, just like you and me. She humbly more than admitted as much herself, "***It is because***

11

I was the poorest and the most ignorant that the Blessed Virgin chose me...if she had found one more ignorant than me she would have chosen her". Bernadette always displayed a deep personal humility. She was a deeply prayerful person (she could recite the Holy Rosary from a very young age and in fact she had her rosary on her person when she encountered Our Lady at the Grotto of Massabielle for the first time. A faith no doubt passed on to her by her parents who were a deeply religious couple.

I could not help thinking of my own late parents, when making role model comparisons with the faith they passed on to me...only in my case I have not lived up to or walked the path of Bernadette. The faith a parent gives to their child **IS** the greatest gift they can ever give their child and their children's children. Faith has been my greatest inheritance from my parents, and for this I am eternally indebted to them.

Before my parents however came their own parents, who too have their own special story which seems to blend in nicely with that of Bernadette Soubirous. My elder sisters narrated to me our family history from past oral accounts they obtained from our elders. My mother's father Sekuru (*grandfather* in my vernacular Shona language) Peter Vakisa, was the first Catholic convert baptised by the Jesuit Missionaries at Gokomere Mission in Zimbabwe around the period 1900. The baptising Jesuit priest named him Peter because he was the *first* Catholic convert at the new Mission station in what is now Masvingo Diocese in Zimbabwe. His younger brother was baptised next and was given the name Andrew (Peter and Andrew being the first followers of Jesus Christ at Capernaum on the shores of the

Sea of Galilee). And his wife Mbuya (*grandmother*)
Catherine Vakisa being another inimitable rock of the faith.

Sekuru Peter Vakisa did not live long, he died young. But
the mustard seed of enduring Catholicism in this good
community and in my family had been firmly sown. Years
later a cousin brother on my mother's side Herman
Nhariwa went on to become one of the early Catholic
priests in Zimbabwe (then Rhodesia). The first born in my
own family also became a Catholic Nun. This mustard seed
sown in the past seemed to be really and truly blossoming.
"*To fall in love with God is the greatest romance; to seek Him
the greatest adventure; to find Him, the greatest human
achievement.*" - **St Augustine** on following God. Other
families in the local Gokomere Mission community also
witnessed successful vocations in their own children.

After the death of Mr Peter Vakisa, the priests took in his
widow *Mbuya* Catherine and her children (who included
my own mother) and gave them accommodation, full
board and education at the Mission until the children
became adults who married to start their own families. The
Missionaries provided them with everything needed for
their lives. So the lives of our mothers and their brother
were totally interwoven with the formative Catholic
Missionary establishment in their local area. The Church
did these wonders for my family.

While Mbuya Vakisa resided at the Mission looking after
her children she was placed in charge of the girls in the
Mission School and became the Boarding Mistress in this
formative Missionary establishment. She taught the girls
Catechism and ensured their proper participation at Mass

and other liturgical events. She also led them in the St Theresa Little Flower Guild for the young girls. Over time however the girls she had mentored would leave the Mission to get married and become young mothers in their own right. Recognising that the Guild she had had for the girls while they were at the Mission became less relevant when they started their new lives as young mothers and housewives, she became instrumental in the formation of the St Anne's Guild (Mbuya Anna) locally and becoming the first Chairperson of that Guild. Her photograph still adorns the St Anne's Guild handbook. Another mustard seed for the faith had just been sown.

Mbuya Catherine had a strict routine of prayers each day even though she had to do her household chores as well as till a small field for her food which in hindsight also doubled up as her physical workout regime to keep her fit. In the community local folks knew that once Mbuya Vakisa started her daytime prayers she would firmly close herself indoors, and any children sent on errands or visitors to her house would have to wait till she was done with her prayers as she would never answer her door in the midst of prayer. My sisters were to tell me that Mbuya Vakisa used to see "visions" in the sky, the most common ones being the "Host", "the Blood of Christ", "Angels" and she did not understand why those to whom she pointed out these things could not see what she was seeing. She had no time for anything that was not Godly. In hindsight her daily prayer routines appear to have coincided with the 3pm Divine Mercy Chaplet, though of course she would not have known about this coincidence which was to come later with the introduction of the Divine Mercy Cahplet. She departed from this world in 1978. We believe she is up

14

there with the Almighty and the angels. With St Bernadette, with Our Lady and all the Saints.

As a young boy I attended boarding school at Gokomere Mission and as a Mass server I would always see my grandmother coming to the early morning Masses even during the cold winter months. I always wondered, and still do, what time she, an elderly person who walked so painfully slowly, would have woken up in order to make it to Mass which started at 6am and sometimes at 5.30am. She would have needed to walk a distance of perhaps about a mile and a half in the darkness of the morning. Mbuya Catherine pray for us. Sekuru Peter pray for us.

My father Edmund Munyengwa and mother Agnes (may they both find eternal peace in the Lord) brought me up into a large devoutly Catholic family, just like themselves. They gave us their children, all they had and dare I say, all that we now have. Without the faith and humble background they gave us in our lives none of us would be where we are today.

Mother and father were materially poor. But they were immensely loving, caring and responsible parents. They taught me to be content with my lot, with anything that I should call mine to always be the sole product of honest hard work. True grit. And so I acknowledge my parents, and their parents, with immense pride, deep conviction and complete contentment. The many weaknesses, transgressions, human frailties and failures both petty and significant, and the very visible numerous blots and dark spots on my sinful life are entirely my own.

15

My views of my parents are also shared by my siblings. On the day our mother passed away in 2009 my eldest sister, Sr Generosa said of our parents, "**Our parents were hardworking, prayerful simple peasants. They were Catholic people who gave their Offertory to the Church as expected. But they went further and gave their very selves, working tirelessly for the Church in any way they were asked or where they saw a need. They gave all their children the gate door to salvation by having everyone of us baptised. They assisted and were very supportive of their daughter who had given herself to the vocations to become a Sister**." "*To give, and not to count the cost; to fight, and not to heed the wounds; to toil, and not to seek for rest; to labour, and not to ask for any reward, save that of knowing that we do Thy will.*" - St Ignatius of Loyola. "*One of the elders then spoke and asked me, 'Who are these people, dressed in white robes, and where have they come from?' I answered him, 'You can tell me, Sir.' Then he said, 'These are the people who have been through the great trial; they have washed their robes white again in the blood of the Lamb. That is why they are standing in front of God's throne and serving him day and night in his sanctuary; and the One who sits on the throne will spread his tent over them…*" (Revelation 7:13 – 15).

Indeed.

And so with great humility, fondness of heart, and utmost appreciation, I could think of no better way to acknowledge and thank these great maternal and spiritual icons in my life than by declaring my gratitude to them in preface to my observations on St Bernadette, who inspires me so much. I am convinced that my forebears would approve. In this way. As what Bernadette's parents did for her, my grandparents and parents seem to have tried to do for us their children.

"Eternal rest grant unto them, O Lord.
And let the perpetual light shine upon them.
And may the souls of all the faithful departed, through the mercy of God, rest in peace. Amen."

Table of Contents

Pope Benedict XVI Presents Heart of Lourdes' Message

APOSTOLIC JOURNEY
OF HIS HOLINESS BENEDICT XVI
TO FRANCE ON THE OCCASION OF THE 150th
ANNIVERSARY
OF THE APPARITIONS OF THE BLESSED VIRGIN
MARY AT LOURDES
(SEPTEMBER 12 - 15, 2008)
**EUCHARISTIC CELEBRATION ON THE
OCCASION
OF THE 150th ANNIVERSARY OF THE
APPARITIONS
OF THE BLESSED VIRGIN MARY
HOMILY OF HIS HOLINESS BENEDICT XVI**
Prairie, Lourdes
Sunday, 14 September 2008

Dear Cardinals,
Dear Bishop Perrier,
Dear Brothers in the episcopate and the priesthood,
Dear pilgrims, brothers and sisters,
"Go and tell the priests that people should come here in procession, and that a chapel should be built here." This is the message Bernadette received from the "beautiful lady" in the apparition of 2 March 1858. For 150 years, pilgrims have never ceased to come to the grotto of Massabielle to hear the message of conversion and hope which is addressed to them. And we have done the same; here we are this morning at the feet of Mary, the Immaculate Virgin, eager to learn from her alongside little Bernadette.

I would like to thank especially Bishop Jacques Perrier of Tarbes and Lourdes for the warm welcome he has given me, and for the kind words he has addressed to me. I greet the Cardinals, the Bishops, the priests, the deacons, the men and women religious, and all of you, dear Lourdes pilgrims, especially the sick. You have come in large numbers to make this Jubilee pilgrimage with me and to entrust your families, your relatives and friends, and all your intentions to Our Lady. My thanks go also to the civil and military Authorities who are here with us at this Eucharistic celebration.

"What a great thing it is to possess the Cross! He who possesses it possesses a treasure" (Saint Andrew of Crete, Homily X on the Exaltation of the Cross, PG 97, 1020). On this day when the Church's liturgy celebrates the feast of the Exaltation of the Holy Cross, the Gospel you have just heard reminds us of the meaning of this great mystery: God so loved the world that he gave his only Son, so that men might be saved (cf. Jn 3:16). The Son of God became vulnerable, assuming the condition of a slave, obedient even to death, death on a cross (cf. Phil 2:8). By his Cross we are saved. The instrument of torture which, on Good Friday, manifested God's judgement on the world, has become a source of life, pardon, mercy, a sign of reconciliation and peace. "In order to be healed from sin, gaze upon Christ crucified!" said Saint Augustine (Treatise on Saint John, XII, 11). By raising our eyes towards the Crucified one, we adore him who came to take upon himself the sin of the world and to give us eternal life. And the Church invites us proudly to lift up this glorious Cross so that the world can see the full extent of the love of the Crucified one for mankind, for every man and woman. She invites us to give thanks to God because from a tree which brought death, life has burst out anew. On this wood Jesus reveals to us his sovereign majesty, he reveals to us that he is

21

exalted in glory. Yes, "Come, let us adore him!" In our midst is he who loved us even to giving his life for us, he who invites every human being to draw near to him with trust.

This is the great mystery that Mary also entrusts to us this morning, inviting us to turn towards her Son. In fact, it is significant that, during the first apparition to Bernadette, Mary begins the encounter with the sign of the Cross. More than a simple sign, it is an initiation into the mysteries of the faith that Bernadette receives from Mary. The sign of the Cross is a kind of synthesis of our faith, for it tells how much God loves us; it tells us that there is a love in this world that is stronger than death, stronger than our weaknesses and sins. The power of love is stronger than the evil which threatens us. It is this mystery of the universality of God's love for men that Mary came to reveal here, in Lourdes. She invites all people of good will, all those who suffer in heart or body, to raise their eyes towards the Cross of Jesus, so as to discover there the source of life, the source of salvation.

The Church has received the mission of showing all people this loving face of God, manifested in Jesus Christ. Are we able to understand that in the Crucified One of Golgotha, our dignity as children of God, tarnished by sin, is restored to us? Let us turn our gaze towards Christ. It is he who will make us free to love as he loves us, and to build a reconciled world. For on this Cross, Jesus took upon himself the weight of all the sufferings and injustices of our humanity. He bore the humiliation and the discrimination, the torture suffered in many parts of the world by so many of our brothers and sisters for love of Christ. We entrust all this to Mary, mother of Jesus and our mother, present at the foot of the Cross.

In order to welcome into our lives this glorious Cross, the celebration of the Jubilee of Our Lady's apparitions in Lourdes urges us to embark upon a journey of faith and conversion. Today, Mary comes to meet us, so as to show us the way towards a renewal of life for our communities and for each one of us. By welcoming her Son, whom she presents to us, we are plunged into a living stream in which the faith can rediscover new vigour, in which the Church can be strengthened so as to proclaim the mystery of Christ ever more boldly. Jesus, born of Mary, is the Son of God, the sole Saviour of all people, living and acting in his Church and in the world. The Church is sent everywhere in the world to proclaim this unique message and to invite people to receive it through an authentic conversion of heart. This mission, entrusted by Jesus to his disciples, receives here, on the occasion of this Jubilee, a breath of new life. After the example of the great evangelizers from your country, may the missionary spirit which animated so many men and women from France over the centuries, continue to be your pride and your commitment!

When we follow the Jubilee Way in the footsteps of Bernadette, we are reminded of the heart of the message of Lourdes. Bernadette is the eldest daughter of a very poor family, with neither knowledge nor power, and in poor health. Mary chose her to transmit her message of conversion, prayer and penance, which fully accord with words of Jesus: "What you have hidden from the wise and understanding, you have revealed to babes" (Mt 11:25). On their spiritual journey, Christians too are called to render fruitful the grace of their Baptism, to nourish themselves with the Eucharist, to draw strength from prayer so as to bear witness and to express solidarity with all their fellow human beings (cf. *Homage to the Virgin Mary*, Piazza di

Spagna, 8 December 2007). It is therefore a genuine catechesis that is being proposed to us in this way, under Mary's gaze. Let us allow her to instruct us too, and to guide us along the path that leads to the Kingdom of her Son!

In the course of her catechesis, the "beautiful lady" reveals her name to Bernadette: "I am the Immaculate Conception". Mary thereby discloses the extraordinary grace that she has received from God, that of having been conceived without sin, for "he has looked on his servant in her lowliness" (cf. Lk 1:48). Mary is the woman from this earth who gave herself totally to God, and who received the privilege of giving human life to his eternal Son. "Behold the handmaid of the Lord; let what you have said be done to me" (Lk 1:38). She is beauty transfigured, the image of the new humanity. By presenting herself in this way, in utter dependence upon God, Mary expresses in reality an attitude of total freedom, based upon the full recognition of her true dignity. This privilege concerns us too, for it discloses to us our own dignity as men and women, admittedly marked by sin, but saved in hope, a hope which allows us to face our daily life. This is the path which Mary opens up for man. To give oneself fully to God is to find the path of true freedom. For by turning towards God, man becomes himself. He rediscovers his original vocation as a person created in his image and likeness.

Dear Brothers and Sisters, the primary purpose of the shrine at Lourdes is to be a place of encounter with God in prayer and a place of service to our brothers and sisters, notably through the welcome given to the sick, the poor and all who suffer. In this place, Mary comes to us as a mother, always open to the needs of her children. Through the light which streams from her face, God's mercy is made

24

manifest. Let us allow ourselves to be touched by her gaze, which tells us that we are all loved by God and never abandoned by him! Mary comes to remind us that prayer which is humble and intense, trusting and persevering, must have a central place in our Christian lives. Prayer is indispensable if we are to receive Christ's power. "People who pray are not wasting their time, even though the situation appears desperate and seems to call for action alone" (*Deus Caritas Est*, 36). To allow oneself to become absorbed by activity runs the risk of depriving prayer of its specifically Christian character and its true efficacy. The prayer of the Rosary, so dear to Bernadette and to Lourdes pilgrims, concentrates within itself the depths of the Gospel message. It introduces us to contemplation of the face of Christ. From this prayer of the humble, we can draw an abundance of graces.

The presence of young people at Lourdes is also an important element. Dear friends, gathered this morning around the World Youth Day Cross: when Mary received the angel's visit, she was a young girl from Nazareth leading the simple and courageous life typical of the women of her village. And if God's gaze focussed particularly upon her, trusting in her, Mary wants to tell you once more that not one of you is indifferent in God's eyes. He directs his loving gaze upon each one of you and he calls you to a life that is happy and full of meaning. Do not allow yourselves to be discouraged by difficulties! Mary was disturbed by the message of the angel who came to tell her that she would become the Mother of the Saviour. She was conscious of her frailty in the face of God's omnipotence. Nevertheless, she said "yes", without hesitating. And thanks to her yes, salvation came into the world, thereby changing the history of mankind. For your part, dear young people, do not be afraid to say yes to the Lord's summons when he invites you to walk in his footsteps. Respond generously to the Lord! Only he can fulfil the deepest aspirations of your heart. You have come to Lourdes in great numbers for attentive and generous service to the sick and to the other pilgrims, setting out in this way to follow Christ the servant. Serving our brothers and sisters opens our hearts and makes us available. In the silence of prayer, be prepared to confide in Mary, who spoke to Bernadette in a spirit of respect and trust towards her. May Mary help those who are called to marriage to discover the beauty of a genuine and profound love, lived as a reciprocal and faithful gift! To those among you whom he calls to follow him in the priesthood or the religious life, I would like to reiterate all the joy that is to be had through giving one's life totally for the service of God and others. May Christian families and communities be places where solid vocations can come to birth and grow, for the service of the Church and the world!

Mary's message is a message of hope for all men and women of our day, whatever their country of origin. I like to invoke Mary as the star of hope (*Spe Salvi*, 50). On the paths of our lives, so often shrouded in darkness, she is a beacon of hope who enlightens us and gives direction to our journey. Through her "yes", through the generous gift of herself, she has opened up to God the gates of our world and our history. And she invites us to live like her in invincible hope, refusing to believe those who claim that we are trapped in the fatal power of destiny. She accompanies us with her maternal presence amid the events of our personal lives, our family lives, and our national lives. Happy are those men and women who place their trust in him who, at the very moment when he was offering his life for our salvation, gave us his Mother to be our own!

Dear Brothers and Sisters, in this land of France, the Mother of the Lord is venerated in countless shrines which thereby manifest the faith handed down from generation to generation. Celebrated in her Assumption, she is your country's beloved patroness. May she always be honoured fervently in each of your families, in your religious communities and in your parishes! May Mary watch over all the inhabitants of your beautiful country and over the pilgrims who have come in such numbers from other countries to celebrate this Jubilee! May she be for all people the Mother who surrounds her children in their joys and their trials! Holy Mary, Mother of God, our Mother, teach us to believe, to hope and to love with you. Show us the way towards the kingdom of your Son Jesus! Star of the sea, shine upon us and lead us on our way! (cf. *Spe Salvi*, 50). Amen.

1 INTRODUCTION

This book is intended for you if you are planning to visit Lourdes, and possibly even other pilgrimage sites or Shrines elsewhere. It is intended to aid your spiritual journey while on pilgrimage as well as give some practical pre-travel spiritual preparations. It is also hoped that it will sign post you to the many areas at Lourdes that you could visit together with other places typically found on a pilgrimage site. But most of all I hope that it will help you to both heighten and deepen your spirituality and help you and me on our journey to the promised land through the loving and warm hands of Our Blessed Mother. You may already have been to Lourdes, or even been many times and simply want to reminisce and retrace your footsteps of that special journey. You may also never have visited Lourdes and with no immediate plans or prospects to make the journey. No matter. You may just want to close your eyes and open your heart to experience a pilgrimage from wherever you may be, whenever this may be.

What triggered my writing this book? Going to Lourdes was a '*light bulb moment*' for me. It ignited a special connection with the place that I had not experienced anywhere else before: the peace, the tranquil, the tangible holiness of this place, and just the place itself whatever time of day, wherever you look and however you look, you see the practical illustration of the mercy and love of God in everyone you see around you as well as the activities taking place there.

When you come to Lourdes you may even be able to see what you decide you want to see. You can also be consumed by the commercialisation of the place by those who have seen marketing opportunities to sell wares and provide commercial services to pilgrims. You may also shut your eyes to these things and find God in this place. Lourdes is for me a personal reminder and testimony to the profound and real Divine Presence that I discovered is freely available there. A reminder to always learn from Bernadette: that to be humble is not to be weak, but that it can instead be the best way to truly become God's child. A reminder that daily God is doing His work in the lives of those who seek Him with sincere hearts. A reminder too that God can work through ANYONE He so chooses, and at Lourdes he chose young Bernadette. That your earthly life can be full of disappointments and miseries and yet be one of God's chosen ones. Lourdes is a message of hope. There I can retreat (and conduct a stocktake) from the unrelenting world of today, a world where Satan and his many manifestations are forever looking for ways to upset and derail the meagre contents of my painstakingly compiled applecart. And in that process disrupting and undermining my fragile confidence, and dishonestly placing seemingly attractive booby traps along my journey towards God's paradise. Lourdes is the gateway to rediscover that I can always go back to God's unlimited mercy, at any time. Yes, always.

Of course, physically going to Lourdes is not the only way to find and experience God's mercy. Nor does it follow that if you go to Lourdes you would automatically find God's mercy, tick-box style. One has to want and yearn for God to enter one's heart. To allow The Holy Spirit do His work as St Alphonsus encourages, "*to allow God to do with you as He pleases...*" Many go to Lourdes but like the camel brought to the oasis, it will drink for the many miles of rough terrain ahead only if it wishes to. The camel minders can only do so much. The camel itself must want to drink the water. Can we turn ourselves into willing camels? Whatever your circumstances Lourdes is a good place to come to receive God's mercy. It is the heart of God's mercy.

2 LOURDES: THE SETTING

Lourdes is a small town in the south of France, about 700 miles from Paris the French capital. The train journey from Paris takes anything from 7 to 10 hours, or a few hours by air. The train gets into Lourdes and shuttle buses are available to ferry pilgrims to their hotels. Or one can take a short taxi ride into the centre of town. If one feels fit enough and travelling light, the distance from the train station to the Sanctuary and hotels is one that can also be walked. There is an international airport outside Lourdes as some pilgrims fly into this holy place via connecting flights from all around the world. Some arrive by coach travelling in groups. Some simply drive. Once in Lourdes most places can be reached on foot, the main pilgrimage areas being within a few square miles of each other. On pilgrimage it can be helpful to plan one's visits, splitting them up for activities for each day for the purposes of making the most of one's time as well as ensuring that each place visited can be done with spirituality, reverence and without haste.

3 CLIMATE

Lourdes' climate is heavily influenced by the surrounding Pyrenees mountains which tower above the town. Lourdes experiences warm summers and generally cool winters.

There can be year-round rainfall but the weather is generally never so severe as to disrupt visitors. Lourdes can be chilly in early spring so it may be a good idea to have long sleeved clothing and coats for visits early in the year till about March. As the season progresses the weather warms up and towards the end of May average daily temperatures of 20°C or even 25°C can be experienced. The months of June, July and August are the busiest in Lourdes, with the flow of pilgrims increasing substantially and higher temperatures being recorded. The fine weather means that visitors can freely explore the Lourdes pilgrimage sites that are described later. It is common to experience rain even in the warm weather, but with plenty of sunshine during most days. Local shops can provide many of the items like umbrellas, light raincoats, jackets etc needed when unexpected weather changes occur. The shops also sell all types of items like candles to light at the candle enclosure, rosaries, statues etc. Most shops stay open daily till around 11pm or midnight when pilgrims can do some shopping after the nightly Torchlight Rosary Procession.

4   THE STORY OF BERNADETTE AND THE MIRACLES OF OUR LADY OF LOURDES (adapted from the Franciscan Media publications, MSM Publications, narrations of various tour guides on visits to Lourdes and various information leaflets from the visitor centre at Lourdes).

The Feast of Our Lady of Lourdes occurs on 11 February each year, coinciding with the first time Bernadette Soubirous encountered "the beautiful lady" at the Grotto of Massabielle. She was born into a very poor family and being the eldest, she took on the responsibility for looking

after and caring for her brothers and
sisters while she was still very young
herself. She had no education
other than the Catholic teachings
which she studied in the evenings.

*" The Casterot family had worked
at the Boly Mill since 1756
and fully intended buying it
one day. But on 1ˢᵗ July
1841, their plans were
dramatically upset when
Justin Casterot was killed in a
cart accident, leaving a wife, four
daughters and a little boy. His widow, Claire, unable to run
the mill alone, decided she must find a man to take over the
lease. Her choice fell upon Francois Soubirous, who worked in
a neighbouring mill and who was still a bachelor at thirty
four. He was invited to court the eldest girl, Bernade, the
"heiress" as was the custom, but against all expectations, he fell
in love with the younger sister, Louise, a pretty sixteen year old
blonde. Francois was so determined that, having tried in vain
to make him change his mind, Claire Casterot eventually
relented. The wedding day was set for November 18ᵗʰ, 1842.
However, only the civil ceremony took place that day, for
Francois had just lost his mother; the church wedding was
postponed until 9ᵗʰ January, 1843.*

*On 7ᵗʰ January 1844, Louise gave birth to a little girl. Two
days later, the child was baptised in the parish church of St
Pierre (which was demolished in 1905). She was christened
Marie Bernade, but would always be known as **Bernadette**.
But the young couple's happiness was soon to be overshadowed*

by misfortune: a tallow candle set fire to Louise's blouse and burnt her breast, leaving her unable to feed Bernadette. So for 18 months the baby girl went to stay with a wet nurse, Marie Lugues, who lived with her husband Basile, in Burg House in the nearby village of Batres. A "wet nurse" was a mother who had just lost her baby and who still had milk that could be fed to another baby.

On 1ˢᵗ April 1846 Francois brought his daughter back home to the mill where Louise was expecting another child. On 17ᵗʰ September she bore a second daughter Toinette. The Soubirous and Casterots were now living eight in 3 rooms. Such overcrowding placed so great a strain on relationships that in 1848, the grandmother decided to take her other children and go to live with her eldest daughter who was now married…Other misfortunes fell upon them. In 1849 Francois was blinded in the left eye by a chip of stone while working on a millstone…In 1852 their financial situation worsened. The mill was sold and the new owner decided to work it himself. …In June 1854, the couple were forced to leave the Boly Mill." (In Lourdes 1844 Bernadette Nevers 1879, p2 – 3, MSM publications. Used with permission)

The story of Bernadette Soubirous is the epitome of humility and love for Christ that has touched hearts for many generations and caused conversion of millions of people from around the world. This story would not be complete if it did not start with the fact that Bernadette is very much a product of the background her parents gave her as a child: a strong and deep faith rooted in the family praying together and with their life wholly immersed in love that Francois and Louise Soubirous, Bernadette's father and mother gave each other and her and her siblings. My view is that the role Louise and Francois Soubirous played has not been adequately acknowledged with the focus primarily mostly always being on Bernadette herself. At her first encounter with Our Lady at the Grotto of Massabielle, we learn that Bernadette could already recite the Holy Rosary as a girl of about 14 years and that she actually had her Rosary on her person on an outing to gather firewood for the family fire. How many young people (or adults?) of this day and age are able to recite the holy Rosary without a prayer book? How many of us are able to publicly display the holy Rosary on our person?

Through Our Lady's impassioned plea for penance, we are reminded in this story that as we are all sinners, that we require God's love and mercy. And love and mercy are found in limitless abundance in God Himself. *'Behold, I stand at the door and knock: if any man hears my voice and opens the door, I will come in to him, and will dine with him, and he with me.'* <u>Rev 3:20.</u> We can find salvation if we humble ourselves like young Bernadette. And through the messages of Our Lady we are called to be witnesses to The Good News. Our ultimate objective is to reach the kingdom of God in heaven. Young Bernadette draws us to the Blessed Virgin Mary, our Mother. Through our Mother we will find the sure route to heaven for where the Mother is, the son will be too. At Calvary Jesus himself gives his mother to us, and reciprocally gives us to his mother. Bernadette continues this theme as she openly shares the messages relayed through her by Our Lady to us. So that we can go to Mary as our Mother with all our joys, and all our difficulties because a mother listens to her children.

My conversations with other pilgrims on various journeys to Lourdes revealed that without exception their testimonials show the beauty of God's mercy in their varied accounts. Each pilgrim who shared their testimonies with me had their trigger moments to their unique "Lourdes experience" in the form of an inner voice speaking to them or an encounter which they experienced. "If *today you hear His voice, harden not your hearts.*" <u>Ps 95:6-7</u>. But as Fr Mark Chikuni CSsR once remarked in a homily: "*we should not always be looking for cause-and-effect processes in prayer for sometimes God simply chooses to remain silent when we ask or are in situations where we seek divine intervention. He does however always respond in His own ways, in His own time. For He knows what is best for us and sometimes what we ask for is **not** what we need*". Bernadette was patient and waited on the graces of God. She knew God's intentions were the best for her. She did not feel humiliated with the instructions to dig up mud to create the spring, nor to drink the muddy water nor to wash in it in the presence of highly sceptical multitudes, some of whom were actually angry with her. God's purpose was above all. Can we put God's purpose above all in the face of humanly embarrassing situations? Do we put God's purpose above our own when we are shielded from open scrutiny by the privacy of being alone or behind closed doors in our homes?

We see in this story that God does some very extraordinary things to those that love Him the most. Like Padre Pio (1887-1968) Bernadette suffers throughout her whole life. Both of them accept their human suffering as the grace that God has granted them. She grows up with the diseases symptomatic of poverty: asthma, physical deficiencies but in the end earns the crown of glorification that only God gives.

5   THE APPARITIONS (adapted from the combinations of various information leaflets, pilgrimage guide narrations at the Lourdes Shrine, the Apparitions texts used with the kind permission of the Direct from Lourdes website (www.DirectFromLourdes.com), the Sanctuaire ND de Lourdes, Pôle Communication (The apparitions (lourdes-france.org) and the booklet *In Lourdes 1844 Bernadette Nevers 1879,* MSM Publications)

The First Apparition Thursday 11ᵗʰ February 1858: The first meeting
After dinner on the Thursday before Ash Wednesday, Bernadette's mother told her children that there was no more firewood in the house. Bernadette and her sister, Toinette and a friend, went to the river Gave to gather some firewood. But to do this they had to cross a canal of cold water.

Hesitating and fearing that she would have an asthma attack, Bernadette stayed on the bank, and the other two girls crossed the stream and picked up wood under the grotto until they disappeared along the Gave river. In her own words Bernadette described the first Apparition as follows, "*I went to the banks of the Gave to gather firewood with two other little girls. They crossed the river and started to cry. When I asked them why they were crying, they said that the water was cold. I asked them to help me throw stones in the water so that I could cross the river without taking my clogs off, but they said I would also have to do as they had done. So I went a little way further on to see if I could find a place to cross without getting my feet wet. I could not so I came back in front of the grotto. Just as I started to take my clogs off I heard a rustling sound. I looked towards the meadow. I could see the trees were not moving at all. I turned back to my clogs. Again, I heard the rustling sound. This time I raised my head and looked towards the grotto. I saw a lady dressed in white: she had a white robe with a blue belt and a yellow rose on each foot, the same colour as the chain of her rosary. When I saw her I rubbed my eyes as I thought I must be mistaken. I put my hand in my pocket to find my rosary. I wanted to make the sign of the cross but I could not lift my hand to my forehead: it fell back down. The Vision made the sign of the cross. Then my hand trembled: I tried again to make the sign and this time managed to. I went through my rosary; the Vision ran her own beads through her fingers, but did not move her lips. When I had finished my rosary, the Vision suddenly disappeared. I asked the other two girls if they had seen anything and they said they had not."* (In Lourdes 1844 Bernadette Nevers 1879, p8 MSM publications. Used with permission.)

On realizing that she alone had seen the apparition, and not her sister or friend, she asked them not to tell anyone what she had seen. Toinette, who was unable to keep a secret, told their mother Louise Soubirous. Bernadette's mother questioned her and forbade her from returning to the grotto again.

The Second Apparition
Sunday 14th February 1858: Holy water

The second time Bernadette went to the grotto (forbidden at first by her mother) was a Sunday and she had felt an inner urge to return there. After Mass her sister and friend asked Bernadette's mother again and she gave them permission to go.

The apparition took place between around midday and about 2pm. After Bernadette had recited the first decade of the rosary the lady appeared. Bernadette asked the lady to remain if she came from God and sprinkled holy water on her (some accounts say Bernadette rather emptied the vial of water into the ground as she did not believe the lady was a bad spirit, causing the 'beautiful lady' to smile). She had collected the holy water from the parish. The lady only replied with a smile and bent her head but did not speak. Bernadette was immobile, and with her eyes fixed on the grotto started to say her rosary. When she finished saying the rosary the lady disappeared. Due to Bernadette now being immobile she was carried back to the mill where she regained full consciousness, and was scorned by her mother "never to return again."

The Third Apparition
Thursday 18th February 1858: The lady speaks for the first time

Bernadette did not return to the grotto on the 15th, 16th and 17th February and no apparitions happened. On the 18th Bernadette was accompanied by some reliable people to the grotto, villagers Jeanne-Marie Milhet and Antionette Peyret. For the first time, on the 18th of February the lady spoke to Bernadette. Bernadette had taken a pen and paper to the grotto and asked the Lady "*what is your name and what is it that you wish from me?*" The lady smiled and said "*It is not necessary for you to write down what I have to say*", but asked Bernadette for a favour "*would you please return for the next 15 days?*". Bernadette agreed. The lady also told Bernadette "*That she could not promise to make me happy in this world, but in the next.*"

The Fourth Apparition
Friday 19ᵗʰ February 1858: The first candle

The 4th apparition happened in the early hours of Friday morning. Bernadette went along to the grotto with her mother, her Aunt Bernarde and 10 other people all holding a candle for protection. Shortly after Bernadette began to pray the Rosary, everyone present noticed that her face became transfigured and illumined. Afterwards Bernadette said that the lady asked her to leave her candle at the grotto. She said she had told the lady "*It's my aunt's and I'll will ask her, and if she say yes, I will.*" This was the origin of the practice of bringing and carrying candles and lighting them in front of the Grotto. There is now the candle enclosure where pilgrims place candles and pray for themselves and their loved ones and for any intentions they bring.

The Fifth Apparition
Saturday 20ᵗʰ February 1858: Silence

On the 5th apparition about thirty people were present, and the news of Bernadette and the apparition was traveling around the village and other towns and people came out of curiosity. Bernadette said that the lady had taught her a new prayer, which she later said she recited every day of her life. The prayer was never repeated or written down and she never revealed it to anyone till her death.

The Sixth Apparition
Sunday 21ˢᵗ February 1858: "Aquero"

This was the first Sunday in Lent with the apparition taking place in the early hours of the morning. A large number of people, over 100 were present and also present was the police on orders of Dominique Jacomet the Police Commissioner. Bernadette as usual recited the Rosary and silently meditated. Afterwards Bernadette was interrogated by Jacomet, and Bernadette's father (Francois Soubirous) told Jacomet, "*I assure you that my daughter will no longer go to that grotto.*" Bernadette would only speak of "AQUÉRO", "that thing" in the local dialect. The Beautiful Lady had told Bernadette on this occasion to "*pray for sinners*". A local physician Dr Dozous told those gathered that he could find nothing abnormal about Bernadette's physical condition even when her mental state was trancelike. He said he found her pulse normal and nothing indicated any abnormality. The next day Bernadette returned to the grotto but the 'beautiful lady' did not appear and some taunted her saying the lady was now afraid of the police and had gone somewhere else safer.

The Seventh Apparition
Tuesday 23ʳᵈ February 1858: The secret

Even though Bernadette was banned from the grotto she returned, keeping her promise and her appointment with the lady. Even more people turned up this time, numbering over 150 people including Jean-Baptiste Estrade (a tax inspector), Duffo from the municipal council, the future mayor of Lourdes, and the officers from the army garrison were present. During the apparition Bernadette's appearance was once more transformed and the men in attendance removed their hats and knelt as a mark of respect. Bernadette appeared intently listening, and then would be joyful, as well as occasionally bowing her head. Asked afterwards she said that the lady had entrusted her 3 secrets that concerned her alone and these too she never revealed to anyone.

The Eighth Apparition
Wednesday 24ᵗʰ February 1858: "Penance!"
The lady spoke to Bernadette entrusting her with a message, asking prayers for penitence, and 200 - 300 people were present. The lady said *"Penance! Penance! Penance! Pray to God for sinners. Kiss the earth as a sign of penitence for sinners!"* The lady also told Bernadette to eat the grass growing below the grotto. From that occasion every time Bernadette visited grotto she repeated the same act.

The Ninth Apparition
Thursday 25ᵗʰ February 1858: The spring

About 300 people were present at the grotto despite the weather being really bad. The lady told Bernadette that she should go and drink the water at the grotto and wash herself there. Seeing none, Bernadette was confused and thought she should go and drink the water at the Gave river. The lady called her back and pointed at a spot just below the grotto to the left. Bernadette started digging with her hands and eating the herbs, and she then uncovered a puddle of muddy water. Bernadette obeyed the lady and

carried on scratching the ground until she was able to drink
some of the water, after the fourth time of disregarding the
muddy water. When the apparition finished Bernadette
said, "*I do not know why the lady disappeared*" and she went
home. The spring began to flow a day later. Until this day.
It has been estimated that pilgrims draw to drink or to take
away in excess of 30,000 gallons of water each day during
the peak pilgrimage season.

The Tenth Apparition
Saturday 27th February 1858: Silence
About 800 people were present and Bernadette repeated
the acts of penitence of kissing the ground on behalf of
sinners and drinking from the spring in her usual position
in front of the grotto. Nothing was said on this occasion.

The Eleventh Apparition
Sunday 28ᵗʰ February 1858: The ecstasy

Over 1,500 people were present. On the second Sunday in Lent, after Mass an unpleasant surprise awaited Bernadette. She prayed, kissed the ground and moved on her knees as a sign of penance. She was then taken to the house of Judge Ribes who threatened to put her in prison and banned once again from the grotto but she replied " *I will never give up.*"

The Twelfth Apparition
Monday 1ˢᵗ March 1858: The first miracle

There were more than 1500 people present. On Monday 1st March, while it was still dark, Catherine Latapie who had come on foot from the neighbouring village of Loubajac arrived at the Grotto. She dipped her paralysed arm in the spring water whereupon it immediately regained full mobility. She hastened to leave, and later that day gave birth to her fourth child, a boy who would become a priest. The healing of Catherine Latapie was the first miraculous healing in Lourdes. The beautiful lady remarked that Bernadette was not using her own Rosary that day, which was true because she had been asked by another lady, Pauline Sans to use her Rosary at the grotto that day.

The Thirteenth Apparition
Tuesday 2ⁿᵈ March 1858: Message to the Priests

The lady spoke to Bernadette and asked her to "*Go, tell the priests to come here in procession with the people and tell them to build a chapel, even a small one.*" Bernadette told this to Fr Abe Peyramale, the Parish Priest of Lourdes. But he was unconvinced and wanted to know the Lady's name. He demanded another test if she was real: to see the wild rose bush flower at the grotto to bloom in the middle of winter.

Fr Peyramale called Bernadette a liar and told her she must never return to the grotto. Then he told her to leave his presbytery. Bernadette did not give up and returned once again with one of the priest's friends and repeated what the lady had told her, "*Go, tell the priests to come here in procession and tell them to build a chapel here.*" Fr Peyramale said "*A chapel! A procession! Poor child this is all what your stories needed*" then in a sharp tone he said, "*Ask this lady her name and when we know it we will build a sanctuary!*"

The Fourteenth Apparition
Wednesday 3ʳᵈ March 1858: A Smile

At about 7 o'clock in the morning Bernadette arrived at the Grotto in the presence of about three thousand people but the vision did not appear. After school, she heard an inner invitation of the Lady. She went to the Grotto and asked her again for her name. The response was only a smile. The Parish Priest told her again: "*If the Lady really wishes that a chapel be built, then she must tell us her name and make the rose bush at the grotto to bloom.*" The rose bush was where the lady stood at the grotto when she came to speak to Bernadette.

The Fifteenth Apparition
Thursday 4ᵗʰ March 1858: The day all were waiting for!

The ever-greater crowd knew that this was the last of the fifteen days that Bernadette had promised the Lady that she would be present at the Grotto and all waited at the end of this fortnight. The vision was silent. Bernadette asked the lady for her name again but the lady only smiled once more. Afterwards Bernadette told the crowd that she would continue to come to the grotto as the beautiful lady had not bid her farewell. Though the crowd had seen her transfigured with a radiance they had not been able to share her experiences and interactions with the lady and had heard nothing of their conversations.

The Sixteenth Apparition (The name they had all been waiting for)
Thursday 25ᵗʰ March 1858: The Immaculate Conception
The sixteenth apparition occurred on the Feast of the Annunciation on 25ᵗʰ March. The vision finally revealed her name but the wild rose bush on which she stood during the Apparitions did not bloom (the one which the parish priest had demanded the lady must make to bloom in the winter as a sign of who she was). Bernadette recounted :
"*She extended her arms towards the ground, then joined them as though in prayer and said* **Que soy era Immaculada Concepciou** (**I am the Immaculate Conception**)". The young visionary left and running all the way to the parish presbytery, continuously repeated these words which she did not understand so that she would not forget them. These words troubled the Parish Priest for he knew that Bernadette could not understand the theological expression nor its meaning nor could she even have possibly heard them before. It had been assigned to the Blessed Virgin only four years earlier, in 1854 by Pope Pius IX who had declared this a Dogma of the Catholic Faith. Bernadette said "*I went for a fortnight and every day I asked the lady who she was, but these questions only made her smile.*" When asked by an onlooker "*are you absolutely certain about this?*" Bernadette replied "*Yes*".

The Seventeenth Apparition
Wednesday 7ᵗʰ April 1858: The miracle of the candle
The town physician Dr Pierre Romaine Dozous watched

the apparitions with some scepticism though he inwardly believed Bernadette and knew her to be genuine and not a person to make up wild stories. He compiled all the evidence together and decided to write a medical journal article explaining that one can have illusions or hallucinations without being insane and that Bernadette was not insane.

The apparition took place between Bernadette and the Virgin Mary about 5 0'clock in the morning with no conversation at all and it was reported that Bernadette seemed to be even deeper than usual in a trance. Since the first time she had been instructed by the lady to bring a candle to the grotto she had always done so. This apparition was witnessed by hundreds of people. This is when the "miracle of the candle" happened. Bernadette was kneeling and saying her usual prayers with her Rosary while holding it in her left hand, and in her right hand a large lit candle. While Bernadette was saying her prayers she suddenly stopped, and joined her right hand with her left hand, the flame from the big candle passing between her fingers as she protected it from the strong breeze around her. The flame from the candle did not burn or make any marks on Bernadette's skin. After 15 minutes or so of this Bernadette made her way to the upper part of the grotto. When Bernadette and the apparition finished Dr Pierre Romaine Dozous asked Bernadette to show her left hand for examination. There was no trace of burning marks on her hands. He then asked another person to hold the candle and light it again and pass it to him. Dr Dozous himself reacted to the candle burning and then put it under Bernadette's hand and she instantly drew her hand away, saying *'You are burning me!'* This was confirmed by hundreds of eye witnesses.

Public access to the grotto was stopped on 8th June in 1858, and trespassing visitors were fined and guards were stationed to protect the grotto.

The Eighteenth Apparition
Friday 16ᵗʰ July 1858 : The Final Apparition
Several months passed and after receiving Holy Communion at Mass on the Feast of Our Lady of Mt Carmel, Bernadette felt an irresistible urge to return to the grotto. The grotto was still barricaded. Bernadette had to take another road to enter the grotto from the other side of the river. Kneeling outside the fence by the riverbank Bernadette said "*I thought I was at the Grotto, like I saw the other times. All I saw was Our Lady. She was more beautiful than ever.*" Kneeling in the grass, in the usual sacred spot, the Immaculate Conception appeared to Bernadette one last time. And the lady did not say anything on this final occasion. The grotto was later reopened to the public in October of 1858 on an order of the Emperor Louis Napoleon III. This was the end of the Apparitions of Our Lady and St Bernadette.

6   REFLECTIONS ON SOME MESSAGES BY OUR LADY (MAI MARIYA) TO BERNADETTE

"Would you come here for a fortnight?" (3ʳᵈ Apparition)
Beyond the message of telling Bernadette to return to the grotto for the next fortnight, there is also a deeper message from Our Lady, calling us all back to God from our sinful ways. The fortnight is also figurative. It can be the usual

47

fortnight, a week, a year, a decade, or a lifetime when this message is referred to us. This is a call to return to the Lord. Our Lady speaks to Bernadette with love, always wearing a smile on her face, with persuasion and compassion in her heart and demeanour. The Blessed Virgin Mary as we know her or as we should know her. She is carrying the message of turning us away from sin, because as the good Mother she is concerned about her errant children - ourselves. The "fortnight" in a sense represents the temporary life that we live here on earth, which if we return to God through Our Lady that "fortnight" will make us worthy of the promises of Heaven.

In another sense this may also represent a sign that Our Lady was already calling Bernadette to prepare herself for the big role she was to play in making Lourdes the special place it has now become. Where people from around the world come and return again and again every "fortnight". Bernadette responded in the affirmative just as Mary did at the Annunciation and then continued to walk in the path of holiness for the rest of her life. Even if you do not physically travel to Lourdes, going to meet Our Lady through prayer, the Rosary, good deeds etc is the commitment to returning to the grotto for the "fortnight" that Our Lady asks of us. Will you and I return to the grotto for a "fortnight"?

"I am the Immaculate Conception" (16ᵗʰ Apparition)
Our Lady takes a long time to reveal herself to Bernadette, only saying who she is on the 16ᵗʰ Apparition, just 2 Apparitions before the last appearance to Bernadette. Persistence such as that shown by Bernadette regarding wanting to know who the *"young lady"* was and her

repeatedly (almost stubbornly) returning to the Grotto to meet her (Aquero) is a big lesson that we must learn from. Our Lady is humble. She does not brag about who she is. She is friendly and always smiles—she always holds and prays the Rosary. But Our Lady is clear about who she is. She states that she is The Immaculate Conception in a confident manner. Unequivocally and leaving no doubt as to who she is. And yet many did not initially believe that it was she who had shown herself to Bernadette. Even the Church took long to believe. In our lives many a time do we not encounter Jesus and do not recognise him? The Gospel of Matthew teaches us, "*Then the righteous will answer Him saying, 'Lord, when did we see You hungry and feed You, or thirsty and give You drink? When did we see You a stranger and take You in, or naked and clothe You? Or when did we see You sick, or in prison, and come to You?' And the King will answer and say to them, 'Assuredly, I say to you, inasmuch as you did it to one of the least of these My brethren, you did it to Me.*" **Mt25:3-40**. Some were jealous that Our Lady showed herself to Bernadette. One of the Sisters in the Convent at St Gildard mistreated Bernadette at Nevers because she was angry that Our Lady had chosen to show herself to a sickly uneducated girl and not to her. Yet Bernadette never begrudged her. In our lives we have to be careful not to be too judgemental of others. For those might just be the instances in which we may be encountering the Lord in the form of the poor people, the sick, the infirm, those of unsound mind, or even those who hate us and give us a hard time. Is it possible that the Lord revisits Lourdes again and again in the form of those multitudes of the bedridden and wheelchair-bound people, those no longer able to speak or help themselves who are all such a common sight at Lourdes? Closer to home does the

Lord not visit you and me each day in the form of the people and situations that present us with unpleasantness, discomfort, dilemmas and all that never seems straightforward in our lives?

"I do not promise happiness in this but the other world" (3rd Apparition)

This is a message to us that we should be looking beyond the worldly things. Jesus too made a similar promise to his disciples, "*You will be sorrowful, but your sorrow will turn into joy*" **John 16:20**. That we must keep straining to win the ultimate prize reserved for those who follow God as taught by St Paul. "*Not that I have already obtained all this, or have already arrived at my goal, but I press on to take hold of that for which Christ Jesus took hold of me. Brothers and sisters, I do not consider myself yet to have taken hold of it. But one thing I do: Forgetting what is behind and straining toward what is ahead, I press on toward the goal to win the prize for which God has called me heavenward in Christ Jesus.*" Philippians 3:12-14. Right up to the end so that one can deserve to say, "*I have fought the good fight, I have finished the race, I have kept the faith.*" (**2 Timothy 4:7**). Our Lady's message is a strong and sobering reminder that "*By the sweat of your face you will eat bread, till you return to the ground, because from it you were taken; for you are dust, and to dust you shall return.*" **Genesis 3:19.**

"Go and drink at the spring and wash yourself there" (9th Apparition)

There were several early miracles that took place at the spring that Aquero showed Bernadette though Bernadette excluded herself saying, "*The spring is not for me.*" People were treated of their ailments and Bernadette once held a candle in her hands with the flames burning through her fingers but without her getting burnt. These miracles of people getting healed by washing at the spring seem to be similar to the many miracles performed by Jesus where people were asked to bath themselves in water, show themselves to the priests and thereby be healed. The practice of washing at the spring has continued, with a huge enclosed bathing area comprising many individual compartments being established a short distance from the spring. Here hundreds upon thousands (perhaps millions) from around the world each year come to bath themselves and pray as part of their Lourdes pilgrimage. The bathing ceremony is a prayerful process as described elsewhere in this book, with every willing pilgrim taking a bath being offered the chance to pray the Hail Mary and other prayers and then saying their intention(s) quietly as part of the bathing rite. Washing at the spring has both physical healing and spiritual dimensions and we will never know the number of the healings that have taken place through going to *"drink at the spring and wash yourself there"*. Some will have undergone true repentance. Others will at last have found the ability to forgive and let go of previous encumbrances from their past. Others perhaps encounter their Damascus here as St Paul did and achieve full and true conversion. Others may experience the contrition they have for so long failed to achieve. Perhaps some are taken from this earth immediately after visiting the baths: perhaps that afternoon, perhaps that evening or the next day. Whenever. But whereupon the words of the pilgrim who said to Sr Generosa at the end of one night's Torchlight Procession, *"Sister, we will meet in Heaven"* find another appropriate occasion for fulfilment as it was unlikely that that evening's chance meeting among the multitudes would ever be repeated on this earth. So too the people of faith who come here never know if it is the last day, but everyone comes in hope. For the mercy of God that resides here.

"Go and eat the grass you will find there" (9th Apparition)

Eating the grass may symbolise doing those things that are unacceptable to us, humbling things or activities. Bernadette ate the grass before huge crowds some of whom were openly mocking her, disapproving or concluding she was mad. Compare this with Jesus being humiliated with arrest, the crown of thorns, the mocking and scourging and eventually being crucified like a criminal at Golgotha. One of the practical actions similar to eating the grass that we can take today may be to show contrition about our transgressions, seeking renewal through the Sacrament of Reconciliation and apologising to those we have wronged. Bernadette had done nothing wrong to deserve to eat the grass at the spring. Yet she did undertake the distasteful act of eating the grass, drinking muddy water and covering her face in it for the repentance of sinners like you and me. Jesus also had done nothing wrong yet he offered his suffering for us on the Cross. In real life, particularly in married life where two people from different backgrounds come together there may be a party who is unrepentant or unwilling to become peacemaker. Sometimes the party who is innocent may have to take on the role of peacemaker, or appearing to be the one in the wrong – for the greater good and offer prayers that God intervenes to make things work. In our daily lives do we accept to eat the grass and drink the muddy water that comes our way? Or can we?

"Go and tell the priests to build a chapel there, even a very small one and bring the people in procession" (14th Apparition)

Spells out the spiritual leadership role of the priests, bishops and the Religious. Our Lady spells out the role of the Clergy as spiritual leaders and who as shepherds must lead their flock to the spring reinforcing the Lord's words. *"But whoever drinks the water I give him will never thirst. Indeed, the water I give him will become in him a fount of water springing up to eternal life."* John 4:14. Only people in harmony can move in unison in procession. The Blessed Virgin Mary is preaching unity to us and moving in one direction towards her son Jesus Christ. A great show of humility in asking for just a small chapel. Today two Basilicas (the Rosary and the Immaculate Conception Basilicas with numerous chapels within them) stand tall magnificently above the spring, and another the St Pius X underground Basilica nearby. The Building of the chapel would enable the priests to celebrate Mass for the people and to allow for The Blessed Sacrament to be exposed there for Adoration. All very thoughtful and prayerful requests made through young Bernadette and which the Church in her wisdom has spared no efforts to implement. So that people can properly experience the Heart of God's mercy that is Lourdes. Lourdes is now blessed with numerous churches and chapels so that the multitudes can worship and meditate.

"Pray God for sinners: Penance, penance, penance" (6th and 8th Apparitions)

The message of repentance is repeated highlighting its importance in order to reach Heaven.

7   REFLECTIONS ON SOME OF ST BERNADETTE QUOTES

(Bernadette quotes from In Lourdes 1844 Bernadette Nevers 1879, MSM Publications and quotes posted at the St Bernadette museum at Nevers)

"I looked at her as much as I could. She looked at me like a person talking to another person." Bernadette talking about the Beautiful Lady whom she also called 'Arquero' underlining the deeply amicable relationship they shared.

"Who do you take me for? I know that if the Blessed Virgin chose me, it's because I was the most ignorant. If she had found one more ignorant than me, she would have chosen her." Bernadette responding to the residents of Lourdes and standing her ground about the genuineness of her encounters with Our Lady…..and her humility in asserting that she was not chosen for any other virtues other than her lowliness and that it could actually have been anyone else. In the face of real opportunities of making a big name for herself, perhaps fame and fortune Bernadette remained firmly grounded in reality refusing to let the chance of instant fame get to her head. How many of us can withstand and resist the worldly temptations in the same way Bernadette did?

"I like taking care of the poor. I like caring for the sick. I'll stay with the Sisters of Nevers." Bernadette shares the strand of mercy and charity that has been carried by many of the saints that we learn about. The sentiment of the poor, the weak, the vulnerable goes back to the Beatitudes, and even prior to that, as preached by Jesus at the Mount of the Beatitudes in Galleria and repeated numerous times

54

in the Holy Scriptures. Bernadette came from very modest origins. But for the majority of us often the inclination is to 'escape' the cycle of poverty when the slightest opportunity presents itself. Many of history's worst rulers and oppressors have generally and typically come from poor backgrounds and their behaviours seem to be those of rebelling against their erstwhile humble origins. This curse did not afflict Bernadette.

"*I'm the broom used by the Virgin. What do you do with a broom after you finish using it? You put it behind the door. That's my place. I'll stay there.*" Self-explanatory unprecedented humility.

"*The grotto was my heaven.*" Referring to how much she loved to go to the grotto and spending time there. This is the grotto at St Gildard, Nevers and Bernadette is said to have remarked that the statue of Our Lady at that Grotto (and which is still there to this day) resembled the most the beautiful lady she used to meet at Massabielle in Lourdes than all the other statues she had seen.

"*I will not forget anybody.*" Reflecting her profound love for others and how therefore serving others was a natural attribute of hers.

"*I thought that God wanted it! When you think that God allowed it, you don't complain.*" Of her lifelong sufferings and illnesses which she never complained about. Despite severe illnesses, pain and visible wounds around her knees she continued to carry out her duties scrubbing Convent floors and other work assigned her in the infirmary until it became physically impossible for her to carry on, without ever complaining.

"The Passion touches me more when I read it than when someone explains it to me."

"I'm not instructed to make you believe it. I'm instructed to tell you about it." Boldly responding to the people she was telling about the messages of her encounters with 'the beautiful lady' and placing the message of Lourdes firmly in their court.

"Jesus alone for a purpose. Jesus alone as a Master. Jesus alone as a guide. Jesus alone for riches. Jesus alone for a friend." Similar to John the Baptist proclaiming, *"He must increase, I must decrease."* **Jn3:30**. The servant must never be greater than the master. This strict and deep sense of service and subservience is perhaps one of the reasons to this day, millions upon millions still flock to the holy Lourdes Shrine.

"Accept each of my tears, each of the cries of my pain, as a supplication for those who suffer, for all those who cry, for those who forget You."

"I am ground like a grain of wheat"
A likely comparison to her being a miller's daughter as her father worked the Bolly mill. Bernadette likens herself to a grain of wheat that is ground into flour. A grain of wheat has nowhere to escape to in the grinding mill and it then becomes a source of life as a food product. It matters not who it will feed as long as it accomplishes its task as a food. This beautiful message calls us to sacrifice our very selves in

carrying out charitable deeds without looking at who the ultimate beneficiaries are. The concept of charity here also invokes the image of the poor woman who stood at the back of the temple and made the offering of the two coins she had without seeking to be noticed.

"If the grain of wheat that has fallen into the earth dies it gives abundant fruit".

As a child of farming parents myself I fully identify with this statement. Bernadette continues with the imagery of a grain of wheat. Quite often we use life examples that are founded in our own backgrounds and what is familiar to us. What is significant is that the grain of wheat that falls to the ground is not wasted but performs a different role to the one consumed as it is still a source of life. In its subsequent life processes it multiplies to produce many more grains which then feed humanity. This is a likely prediction about herself, as what was to happen when she had died would end up with so many people now visiting the Holy Shrine of Lourdes and the conversion that goes with it. "*And as soon as the grain is ready, the farmer comes and harvests it with a sickle, for the harvest time has come.*" Mk4:29. After her life Bernadette has become "abundant fruit."

"He is all I need"

An exhortation that we should not seek too many things in life but to be content with seeking God only. St Alphonsus encourages us, "*Let your constant practice be to offer yourself to God, that He may do with you what He pleases...Since His delights are to be with you, let yours be to be found in Him.*"

"We must love without measure"

We must never doubt God, or ask what we will get in return. Former US President JF Kennedy famously remarked, "*Ask not what your country can do for you, but what you can do for your country.*" Loving without measure also implies infinite forgiveness, unconditional forgiveness, boundless love.

"Jesus alone for Master"
We must not have any other masters. Nor go to false prophets, so numerous these days and who passionately and shamelessly preach the gospel of earthly prosperity as they exploit those who gullibly throw the very little material possessions they have at these false prophets. Also do not consider yourself the master even if things are going well for you. You must always know who gave you that which you have today. All of Bernadette's pronouncements are expressions of humility, putting God first above all else. Another element in Bernadette is not giving up. She was not at first believed but persisted. We see constructive persistence, repeatedly returning to the Grotto despite family and community disapproval and cynicism.

Another element in Bernadette is coping with adversity. She lacked formal education, was herself of poor health and came from a family experiencing depressed social and economic circumstances. She was sent off away from her family first as a baby to be wet nursed and later as a young girl to work so the family had "one less mouth to feed" and yet she did not disconnect from the family or harbour bitterness as she grew up. Being sickly from birth, publicly humiliated at the Grotto, and tested by Our lady in various ways including having to eat grass and drink muddy water in public do not appear to have negatively affected her.

"I have come to hide myself (with Jesus Christ for God)"
Bernadette spoke of her move to Nevers, away from the
publicity that Lourdes had given her. It is said that when
she entered the Convent of St Gildard at Nevers, for the 13
years she was there she never left till her death even when
Francois her beloved father or her mother died. Once a
news reporter went to Nevers Convent seeking to interview
her. She inadvertently answered the gate and when the
reporter asked for her she told him to wait so she could go
and call Sr Marie Bernade as she was by then called. She
then asked another Sister to go to the gate to attend to the
reporter and stayed away from the inquiring newsman. She
had come to Nevers to hide herself and be with Christ.

"Help me to thank God to the very end"
It is also a warning not to fail at the last hurdle. A word of
caution for us all. As highlighted in Revelations about the
glory of God. There are many who lead lives of
righteousness only to then throw all the good work away at
the very end.

***"Holy Mary, Mother of God, pray for me a poor
sinner..."*** Then Bernadette asked for a drink. Having made
sign of the Cross, she swallowed a few sips of water, bowed
her head, and went to eternal sleep in the afternoon on
16th April 1879, the Wednesday just after Easter.

8   A DAY AT LOURDES: PLACES TO VISIT AND THINGS TO DO

Some fly into this Holy Place into Lourdes airport. Some arrive by train, some by coach travelling in groups. Some simply drive. Numerous local hotels in Lourdes offer pilgrim packages for daily or several days' stay. There are many hospitals, hospices and places that care for the many hundreds of thousands of sick and disabled people who come here.

Most places around Lourdes can be reached on foot, the main pilgrimage areas perhaps being within a few square miles that can be walked. It can be helpful to plan one's visits, splitting them up for activities for each day for the purposes of making the most of one's time as well as ensuring that each place visited can be done with spirituality and reverence.

On a typical morning you can wake up early and make your way to the Grotto of Our Lady to pray. The Grotto is open and accessible at any time. During the day there are usually long queues of people wanting to visit the water spring within the Grotto, considered by many to be the most sacred place at Lourdes. Those on wheelchairs and stretcher beds are given direct access to the spring so that they are not kept waiting.

Starting the day with breakfast at one's hotel and one can then go away for the day or one can make an early visit to the grotto and return to the hotel for breakfast between 630am and 9am. Lunch is served in the hotels at 12 noon and dinner at 7pm. Most hotels offer three full meals per day: breakfast, lunch and dinner.

In 2015 when I visited with my sister a nun, Sister Generosa she asked that I cancel the lunch option from our breakfast-lunch-dinner hotel package: "*We have come here to pray and not to enjoy worldly comforts!*" she admonished. "*It will suffice that we have only breakfast and dinner. You know my brother, when you are on pilgrimage one of the elements of it is your self-giving, fasting so you can draw yourself to God and show that you want to suffer with and for Christ.*" I was already into several lessons since we started off from our initial rendezvous in Paris, me coming in from Essex, England and she arriving direct from Zimbabwe. One of many lessons I was to learn from my then 73 year old sister who has spent all her life serving God. At meals we would take turns to say grace and afterwards have the post meal prayer before leaving the restaurant. With Lourdes being a wholly Catholic place, hotel waiting staff would always stop and pray with us if they were bringing in food or collecting crockery as we ate. After breakfast we would go to Sister's room to pray and read the day's Readings for the start of a good day and to dedicate everything we do that day to the Lord.

Morning Mass

After breakfast we make our way to the St Cosmas and St Damian Chapel where there is an English Mass every day at 9 am except on a Sunday or Wednesday when there would be an International High Mass in the 25,000 seater Pope Pius X underground Basilica. The Mass in the St Cosmas and St Damian Chapel lasts less than 1 hour and is normally concelebrated by two priests. The International Mass in the Basilica takes close to two hours and is usually concelebrated by a Cardinal or Archbishop with hundreds of priests, deacons and Mass servers. Always full to capacity and a truly memorable experience. There are also programmes for Masses in other languages in the Basilicas and the numerous chapels each day. Some of the Masses are specifically arranged for the groups of pilgrimages who come to Lourdes and the pilgrimage organisers prearrange Masses for their pilgrimage groups in addition to the many other common Masses taking place each day.

Various options of places to visit

Following Mass we can go to the Visitor information Centre to get information about places to visit. And we can visit any of the numerous places such as the Rosary Basilica, the Immaculate Conception Basilica, The Grotto, The Baths, the Adoration Chapel, St Bernadette's chapel, The High Stations of The Cross. Sr Generosa tells me during our pilgrimage that EVERY Holy place has Stations of the Cross, and one should not complete a pilgrimage without doing The Stations of The Cross. At Lourdes we do these one rainy morning as we are coming to the end of our time at Lourdes as we will not leave without doing these, especially at Lourdes. On the day we have planned to go to The Stations of The Cross, it literally stops raining as we come out of morning Mass and we are just discussing how we will make the Stations of The Cross in the heavy rain. Yesterday it was raining so heavily we had to adjust our programme of the day to visiting only indoor places such as the Adoration Chapel, the Rosary Basilica and watching the St Bernadette video in the information centre. Our Lady seems to be in charge of everything that happens here and has been listening to our intentions and this is just one of many things that happen here if you listen to the Mother's quiet and gentle voice. She has just cleared the way for us to do The Stations of The Cross.

Daily Benediction

At 5pm each day there is Benediction in the Pope Pius X Basilica. It is possible to join the Benediction procession on its way to the Basilica or you may go to the Basilica in advance to await the arrival of the procession and participate in the Benediction. At the end of this you can go to your hotel for dinner or stroll into the shops, many of which remain open till about 11 pm to allow pilgrims who have spent the day visiting places or praying an opportunity to pick up some of the many merchandise items and sacramentals that are available in Lourdes. Prices across the shops can vary widely though many are quite comparable and the quality of items is generally very good. And you constantly hear affectionate references to "*Santa Bernadette*" in every shop. With the shopping experience generally being a very prayerful act in itself.

Later in the evening at 9pm the daily Torchlight procession begins at the Rosary Basilica. It starts at and ends there an hour or an hour and half later with a blessing. Pilgrims then retire to their hotels to rest and start another day of pilgrimage the next morning.

The Grotto

You can sit or kneel at the Grotto, gazing at the grotto, meditating in silence and emptying yourself, praying The Rosary, spending a quiet peaceful time connecting with Our Lady at the place where she appeared to Bernadette and watching the spring water seeping out of the mountainside. Or simply resting. You can also go to the Grotto during the scheduled Rosary sessions. The grotto is a public place for anyone.

The Immaculate Conception Basilica and chapels

The Immaculate Conception Basilica is built behind the Rosary Basilica right next to it but higher up the mountain.

The Rosary Basilica

On the west side of the square is the Rosary Basilica, with two small towers. It was built in 1889 and holds about 4,000. Inside, there are 15 chapels dedicated to the mysteries of the rosary (before The Luminous Mysteries). Outside the Rosary Basilica is the Parade or Esplanade or Piazza, a large open space where the Torchlight Procession begins and ends each night. People come into the Rosary Basilica to pray the Rosary or to just meditate. Sometimes you may notice a soul sitting quietly gently and peacefully napping. Perhaps it is the exertions of their programme which has led to fatigue or they are unwell. Try not to judge them. But whatever the case they are in the right company here with Our Lady, who will look after her son or daughter who has given up time to be in her presence. The painted walls of the interior of the Basilica are done very beautifully. On the outside of the Basilica on the right hand side as you face the Rosary Basilica is the Grotto. So the Rosary Basilica is built almost above the spring. Both the Rosary Basilica and the Immaculate Conception Basilica stand above the spring. The Lady said to Bernadette: "*Go and tell the priests to build a chapel there, even a very small one and bring the people in procession.*" Well, two Basilicas for one small chapel requested.

The Reconciliation Chapel

Perhaps one of the first places to visit on arrival. For confession. "*Penance,*

Penance, Penance". To free one's soul for the pilgrimage. To find peace and receive the Sacrament of absolution. Confessions are available all day at the Chapel of Reconciliation not far from the Grotto and the Rosary Basilica. Conducted by many priests in many different languages.

The Crowned Virgin Statue on the Esplanade
The Crowned Virgin statue reminded me of the beautiful and popular song Ndiri mwana waMariya (*"I am Our Lady's child"*). "*The best and most beautiful things in the world cannot be seen or even touched - they must be felt with the heart.*"- **Helen Keller.** This sums up the beauty of the statue gracing the centre of the Esplanade. More than just beauty. It signifies the Immaculate Heart of Our Lady.

A widely held legend at Lourdes is that if you place a rose at the Crowned Virgin statue in the centre of the Esplanade (Parade), Our Lady will call you back to Lourdes and you will definitely return. I placed a rose at her feet on my first visit in 2014. I have come back and am happy to become an addition to this legendary story. This year I plan to place two or more roses at her feet. Another legend is that the artist making the statue being non-Catholic had placed her rosary in her left hand. The next morning after its placement on the Esplanade the rosary was found to have been miraculously swapped over on to the right hand.

The Torchlight Procession

Thousands of people (maybe five, ten, fifteen or twenty thousand or more) line up each night for this procession, some queuing for hours before the 9pm start time: the bed-ridden being pulled along by the volunteers, those in wheelchairs being wheeled along by those looking after them, parents with children, young couples, everyone. The sight of all these people is itself a miracle and an experience to behold. There are also those with no visible physical scars. We all line up together, with those in wheelchairs and stretcher beds being given preference at the front. We light up our candles, tradition here being that the light is passed on along person to person starting from those that will lead the procession carrying the beautiful statue of Our Lady. To protect the candles from the wind each candle has a yellow, white or blue cover on which is printed some of the hymns sung along the way such as 'Immaculate Mary', 'Salve Regina' used during the procession etc. The cover apart from protecting the candles from the wind, also signifying the cupped hands Bernadette held over the candle without it burning her during one of the apparitions.

The procession takes place each night at 9pm, its route about a mile long starting way before the Rosary Basilica depending on the numbers participating each day and then going all the way up to the St Michael's gate and snaking its way back to the Rosary Basilica. Some of the sick can speak for themselves. Others not. Some are not in a state to be self-aware any more. But they line up in the queue of the Torchlight procession minded by those who bring them there. Hope. The Procession is a slow and unhurried prayer journey.

People are encouraged to pray and sing in their own languages, reliving the spirit of Pentecost. In fact the rosary itself

is conducted in as many languages as can be fitted in by those volunteering to lead each night. Camaraderie amongst Pilgrims of all nationalities, and it seems you are able to understand the language of another from a country you have never been to.

Lighting Candles in the enclosure

At the fourth apparition Bernadette said that the lady asked her to leave her candle at the grotto. She said "*It's my aunt's I'll ask her, and if she says yes, I will.*" Bernadette came to the Grotto with a lighted blessed candle. This became the origin of bringing and carrying candles and lighting them in front of the Grotto and in the candles enclosure.

You can buy candles of all sizes from the very smallest to some very big ones that may need to be carried by two or more people together! You then take these to the candles enclosure where you can light them and say some prayers aloud or silently and leave them there to burn out completely. This is a very popular site with pilgrims and sometimes looks like some kind of fire site due to the large number of candles merrily burning away there at the same time. The desire to light candles and their sheer numbers mirror the many reasons that pilgrims come here. The many things for which people come here seem partly reflected by the intentions expressed in the candles being lit here.

On visits to Lourdes I always buy candles and take them to light them in the candles enclosure. If you wish, before lighting your candles you could ask any of the multitudes of priests always in sight and to bless you with your candles. It does not matter that the priest does not speak your language, they will always understand your request and pray and bless you and your candles. God understands any language on this earth that He created.

The Adoration Chapel

In silent prayer and long hours of kneeling the Sisters here take turns to keep continuous vigil in front of The Blessed Sacrament. The Very Real Presence of The Blessed Sacrament is in every Adoration. And here in Lourdes how cannot the Son be where His mother is? On the very first day of our pilgrimage with Sr Generosa, after the morning Mass she said the first place we had to go to was the Adoration Chapel. I had shown her a visitors' programme that I had printed off the Lourdes website prior to coming here. So we headed to the Adoration chapel. We got inside and being a Sunday the Chapel was full and we had to wait in the entrance way for some pilgrims to make their way out before we could get in to find some space inside. When we eventually got in, we knelt down and prayed before The Blessed Sacrament. It was where we spent most of the Sunday afternoon. Sr was in no hurry to go anywhere else. I had had several other places in mind for us to visit that

71

afternoon. Despite the fact that I had been to Lourdes before and knew the geography and the places we could go to in an order that I had prepared in my mind, Sr seemed to know exactly what to do and in what order for the next ten days. I began to understand. My sister has spent all her life serving God and knows something about these things. On this first day when we left the Adoration Chapel it was already time to go for the Benediction at 5pm in the Pope Pius X underground Basilica.

The Baths

The Baths are open daily and are just a short walk from the Grotto. *"Go and drink at the spring and wash yourself there."* There are two sections, one for men and the other for women. You wait in the queue and when your turn comes you change clothes and after undressing you enter a Bath cubicle with only a towel wrapped around you. Together with the attendants who seem to be highly multilingual they ask what language you speak and you recite the Hail Mary together in one of the languages that you agree with them. They give you a few moments to silently say your intention(s). You are then dipped in the bath full of icy cold water coming directly from the spring. While in the water you can pray quietly and say your intention(s) silently through Our Lady for her intercession on your behalf. I found this to be a remarkable experience. I always felt I had cast away a heavy load from both my body and my heart. The spring water washing away my sins and my inner hurts. I felt a new person. On occasions I would make time to visit the baths more than once during the same pilgrimage. And promised Our Lady not to go back to sin like before.

The sick are brought in through separate extra entrances in order to respect their frail conditions, one for men and another for women. A large number of the sick on their sick beds, in their wheelchairs, on crutches accompanied by their angel like volunteer chaperones. If people make noise at the Baths they are reminded not to do this at the baths. Sometimes the rosary is recited for everyone to participate. It is a most prayerful place. Some hold their rosary in silent prayer while in the queue. I already have mine in my hands and as it is Tuesday afternoon, I recite the Sorrowful Mysteries. The baths are one of the key places that pilgrims plan to visit during their stay at Lourdes. Many have come from far, some are here for the first time to have a lifetime opportunity to be cleansed at the Baths. There are also times when the Rosary is recited communally by all the pilgrims waiting to go into the baths.

The Sorrowful Mysteries that I am reciting mirror the atmosphere here at the Baths. The sick and infirm are already making a massively long queue that extends as far as the Grotto about 200 yards away. I ask one of the assistants if this is always the case every day. "*Si si, it is like this all days!*" the man helpfully replies. "*Sometimes more,*" he adds. He looks up, "*Santa Bernadette and Our Lady.*" I nod in understanding and thank him. I go to a desk nearby and look at the piles of flyers neatly arranged there. I see that they are in several different languages but look to be similarly formatted. There is a pile of flyers in English. I take one and ask the assistant I spoke to a few minutes and gesture to him if it is alright to take one. "*Si, si!*" he encourages me. I bow in appreciation and take my place back in the queue. The men on either side of my queue move to provide me with a place to sit, tacit acknowledgement by them that I was sitting with them before and am not jumping the queue.

The people who have come here, both those seemingly in good health and those on stretchers and sick beds touch my heart. Each is hurting somehow, like I was. They have a purpose to be here. All need God's mercy. Redemption. A reprieve. Renewed hope. Their physical condition might improve. Maybe not. I ask myself what may be going on in their minds, in their hearts. Are some looking beyond this world and focussing *"on the other world"* where Our Lady promised Bernadette happiness? The sick and the sound find a common denominator here. All of us need something that only God can give. Mercy. They have come to the right place, to the heart of God's mercy. Lourdes. But no one knows if the many miracles that everyone heard about since they came here will apply to them. *"When they had gathered together they asked him, "Lord, are you at this time going to restore the kingdom to Israel?"* He answered them, *"It is not for you to know the times or seasons that the Father has established by his own authority. But you will receive power when the Holy Spirit comes upon you, and you will be my witnesses in Jerusalem, throughout Judea and Samaria, and to the ends of the earth."* (**Acts1 v 6 – 8.**)

The High Stations of the Cross and The 28 steps

I will go to the High Stations of the Cross up the mountain top where if you wish you can do these using the standard narrative or replacing them with self-examination meditation prayers and questions about our everyday lives, works and relationships which give a very powerful relevance with God and with others as I make renewal commitments about my life.

At the place where the High Stations begin, there are 28 steps that ascend to the first Station of the Cross. Many people including myself like to kneel at these steps one at a time and recite some prayers and some special intention and then rise one step at a time and do other prayers and ask for another intention. And so on. This is a special way of self-giving and sacrificing oneself and suffering as our Lord did carrying and later crucified on the Cross. It can take close to an hour to finish the 28 steps, following which one may be in much pain. This pain can last the rest of the day or even several days if one is not used to regular exercise. One can then go on the rest of The Stations of the Cross. I have now found it better to do the Stations and then come back to do the 28 steps. In 2015 whilst Sr Generosa and I were at the foot of the 28 steps, a lady came and joined us in silent prayer. She then climbed up the steps to the top. And then she did the most wonderful thing. She opened the large bag that she had and took out a large quantity of the loveliest bouquet of flowers and laid them at Jesus' feet. She knelt down to pray and then she left. What a most thoughtful and prayerful thing to do! At the First Station of The Cross.

9   THE TESTIMONIES

The Church to date has recognised about 70 miracles at Lourdes. *"These are physical manifestations. But how many spiritual miracles and others unknown have taken place there? We may never know…"* **Fr Pasquino Panato, Our Pilgrimage leader, May 2014.**

A Eucharist Miracle
(Lourdes July 1997)
Always awe struck, have I heard or read of episodes on the Real Presence;
Yet nothing compares with a first-hand experience as at St Joseph Chapel in Lourdes;
When, as the bell struck for communion and communicants trooping towards the altar;
Behold! A lady visibly in tears at the joy of meeting the Eucharist Lord for the umpteenth time!
© Benjamin Takavarasha

Her speech was restored on arrival at Lourdes
On 2nd May 2014, on my first pilgrimage to Lourdes we travelled by coach for one and a half days from England with a lady from our neighbouring sister parish who had lost her voice at Christmas the previous year. She was unable to speak all along the way and could only whisper in conversation. Until she whispered her condition to us, we had all been wondering if she was suffering from a severe cold or flu. As we arrived in Lourdes, setting sight on approach to the town beneath us in the valley, she suddenly got her voice back and was able to speak again for the very first time since we had met her. She literally regained her voice the very moment we set sight on Lourdes town as we

made the final approach. Like me it was also her first time to come to Lourdes on pilgrimage. This both surprised and inspired us all as we began our pilgrimage. The lady concerned was simply happy to have been cured at Lourdes. This was my first direct encounter with the works of Our Mother of Lourdes.

The Testimony of Christine

On 11 February 2021, on the Feast of Our Lady of Lourdes I attended the live streamed Mass beamed from the Shrine of Our Lady of Walsingham, Norfolk in England. As part of his homily the celebrating priest Fr John Delaney shared a testimony by someone he knows and who had given their permission for that testimony to be shared, hence its use during the homily. Immediately after the Mass my brother Benjamin who also followed the same Mass called me and says, "*Did you follow this Mass?*" I said yes, because I already knew what he was going to talk about as in any case we both normally follow the Walsingham Masses during the COVID-19 pandemic. Afterwards I contacted Walsingham Shrine and after a few days Fr John who had celebrated that Mass got in touch with me. After a few days I was able to get a copy of Christine's testimony and her permission to use it verbatim, so here goes:

"In 1995 I was asked by a friend to accompany her on her parish pilgrimage to Lourdes. At that time I was enduring considerable pain from a condition that had not yet been properly diagnosed and so decided it would be a good idea to join her. On arrival in France I was immediately struck by a flare-up of my stomach ulcer and was unable to eat anything other than bread rolls and milk for the duration of our 7 day stay in Lourdes.

I decided that I should go into the waters and it was whilst queueing to enter the baths that it came to me that I would be very selfish asking for healing for myself when my brother John (not the priest) was at home in England suffering from terminal cancer. So I entered the bath with the words "Not for me Lord, but for John" on my lips. I gasped for air as I entered the freezing waters with the shock of the unexpected iciness. However as I came out of the water I was immediately dry without the need of a towel.

To give you some idea of my brother John, he was only in his fifties and had everything to live for but he had expressed to me on more than one occasion that he wished he had my faith. He was not of the Catholic persuasion and said that he just didn't know what to believe. How he wished he had the faith that he saw in me.

Eight weeks after my immersion into the waters of Lourdes my brother John died. My heart broke and I believed I had wasted a chance of healing through asking too much of the Lord.

As I sat in the crematorium saying my final farewell to John the minister who was a childhood friend throughout John's school years began to speak. "I am not going to talk about John" he said "Because you all knew him I am going to read you a letter John wrote eight weeks ago instead." In this letter John asked us not to grieve too much for him. He said '*I do not know if there is a God, but I believe. Or if this man Jesus really lived, but I believe. I don't know if the teachings of the Church are right, but I believe. I know nothing about this place called Heaven but I believe in it and if what I believe is true we will all be together one day. So do your mourning but then go on with your lives and be happy. I will wait patiently for the day when we will all be together again and for eternity.'*

The healing of Lourdes had not been a physical one but a spiritual healing. Our Lord knew better than me what was needed and gave John the greatest gift of healing. He gave him faith that he may go into the beyond with confidence in the mercy of God.

I left the crematorium with tears of joy mingled with tears of sorrow and with a grateful heart for favours received. I have since learned that nothing is too much for the Lord. Blessed be God.
Christine"

The young angels
On arrival at Lourdes I often like to take a late-night walk before retiring to bed. Not to go into the bars, but to go to the grotto to tell Our Lady that I have come. To meet her at her sanctuary, the grotto.

Tonight several bars are still open. Streams of young people from their late teens to perhaps the mid-30s fill the streets still in their volunteer or pilgrimage group uniforms. At this late hour they will already have helped their charges to bed in their various hospitals and hotels and are themselves heading to their own hotels to get some rest ahead of another busy day tomorrow ferrying the sick and elderly to the many sites and activities that fill each day at Lourdes. There are many of them. I keep walking. There are scores of other young people chatting merrily, some having drinks. They all seem jovial. Some are speaking in English, French, German and other languages I do not recognise. Seeing all these young people who seem connected with the voluntary work around Lourdes somewhat eases my erstwhile fears about the Church of the future. Where I live in England the Church only sees a small number of young people coming to Mass and participating in Church activities.

The Holy Father's call to us to evangelise in a thousand different ways seems to have been heeded by these young people I see before me. Perhaps the Church does have a future after all. Here the Holy Spirit is at work. Or at play. The young people are doing what young people do, hanging out with their friends, sharing banter. Except the groups of young people I see have purpose. They have either come to Lourdes supporting elderly or sick people, or they have come here to spend time as helpers enrolled on the many charities whose work helps to make a pilgrimage to Lourdes a special event for those who would otherwise not be able to come here on their own. Some are also part of a pilgrimage group from their own parish or diocese.

I walk towards St Joseph's Gate, one of the two main entrances to the Sanctuary of Our Lady, the place where St Bernadette used to come to meet with Our Lady. It is now half an hour after midnight. For the first time in my visits to Lourdes, I find this gate closed and so cannot access the Sanctuary. I am disappointed but I quickly reflect on some of the recent events of random bombings and killings across the globe. The Church is taking steps to respond to this changing world. Even the Holy Sanctuary has to close too to be reopened tomorrow morning when it is daylight, as a safety measure. I say a quiet night prayer as I slowly walk back to my hotel to retire for the night. I will come back in the morning. I have not been able to get to the grotto but the young volunteers are perhaps who Our Mother wanted me to see tonight and to appreciate their devout ministry. I am content now to go back to the hotel and retire. Lessons abound everywhere here as long as you keep your eyes and mind open to them. These young people have been my grotto tonight.

Volunteers ("Upon their shoulders are Angel wings")
Lourdes is always teeming with volunteers. I have never before seen or witnessed a sight like this. Thousands upon thousands of wheelchair bound or stretcher bed ridden people being moved around morning, afternoon and night. Up and down, coming and going. All chaperoned and pulled or pushed by willing and smiling faces. All nationalities, ages and genders and conditions of infirmity. Volunteers abound in all walks of life at Lourdes. Volunteers with the sick. Some bring the sick to Lourdes and some simply come to Lourdes to meet and take care of them here, giving up a part of their lives and freely offering it to others. They come from Malta, France, Switzerland, the UK and many parts of the world. To help humanity. To find God. To find themselves. To find mercy. To find forgiveness. Their reasons for being here may never all be known but what they do is Godly.

The Parable of the Good Samaritan comes to mind. *"But because he wished to justify himself, he said to Jesus, 'And who is my neighbour?' Jesus replied, 'A man fell victim to robbers as he went down from Jerusalem to Jericho. They stripped and beat him and went off leaving him half-dead. A priest happened to be going down that road, but when he saw him, he passed by on the opposite side. Likewise a Levite came to the place, and when he saw him, he passed by on the opposite side. But a Samaritan traveller who came upon him was moved with compassion at the sight. He approached the victim, poured oil and wine over his wounds and bandaged them. Then he lifted him up on his own animal, took him to an inn and cared for him. The next day he took out two silver coins and gave them to the innkeeper with the instruction, 'Take care of him. If you spend more than what I have given you, I shall repay you on my way back.' Which of these three, in your opinion, was neighbour to the robbers' victim?' He answered, 'The one who treated him with mercy.' Jesus said to him, 'Go and do likewise."* **Luke 10 29-37.** Everyday, every week, every month every year thousands of volunteers come to Lourdes to live the parable of the Good Samaritan. I spoke to some of these volunteers during my pilgrimages. They are a cheerful collection and many have other professions than caring for patients but they come to Lourdes to do God's bidding as part of their devotion to help others.

The volunteers are visible everywhere around Lourdes in the company of those they care for. If you slow down or stop to watch them you see that they are talking to the people they look after, singing for them, smiling and showing them sights as they get around taking them to all the special places around Lourdes – to Mass, the Baths, the Grotto, the Chapels, everywhere. Sometimes they stop to enable their charges a moment to take in the significance of a particular site or landmark. Patiently and unhurried. The terrain around Lourdes is one of steep ascents and descents as this is a hilly area. You are either ascending steeply or sharply descending. It is tiring to just be walking around on your own without carrying any ware. It must therefore take quite some effort for the volunteers who include elderly men and women, young men and young women alike to pull or push wheelchairs in this terrain but to always wear smiles on their faces, with good road manners exuding what I consider to be the graces of angels sent straight down from heaven to this wretched earth. This is my impression of these holy people, who often patiently wait in long queues with the people they are transporting around or attend Mass with them, sometimes in the scorching, blazing and dazzling hot sun or drizzling showers. Michael Jackson's vision of "...*the world must come together as one...to lend a hand...to make a brighter day*" in his masterpiece song *"We are the world"* seems not far-fetched. This sight of the volunteers is one that preaches its own Gospel. I marvel at the great vision of Our Lady who must have foreseen all this when she smiled and coaxed little Bernadette to return to the grotto repeatedly. And marvel too at Bernadette Soubirous herself for always saying to herself that *"Perhaps I have not yet suffered enough..."* *"The spring is not for me."* So that others would be saved. That if others would be saved because of her suffering, then her pains were nothing in comparison...perhaps that is what she meant. The old country singer Conway Twitty may as well have been singing of the Lourdes volunteers when he prophesied (I paraphrase) *"Upon your shoulders there's a pair of angel wings. Life with your assistance and support is like living in a beautiful dream."*

The sheer numbers of young people on a diocesan pilgrimage

"They shall mount up with wings like eagles, they shall run and not be weary, they shall walk and not be faint." **Is40:31.** The sight of the volunteers at Lourdes is a great evangelisation, a preaching of the Gospel through deeds. David O Mckay captures this beautifully, *"I'd rather see a sermon than hear one any day. I'd rather have one walk with me than merely point the way."* In *Evangelii Gaudium* The Holy Father Pope Francis continues this theme, *"...this mission demands great generosity on our part, it would be wrong to see it as a heroic individual undertaking, for it is first and foremost the Lord's work, surpassing anything which we can see and understand...in every activity of evangelisation the primacy always belongs to God who has called us to cooperate with Him and who leads us on by the power of His Spirit...this conviction enables us to maintain a spirit of joy in the midst of a task so demanding and challenging that it engages our entire life."* © Libreria Editrice Vaticana

On one occasion we attended a Mass led by the Diocese of Salford, which is in England near Manchester which comes to Lourdes annually on pilgrimage. This Diocese had a large number of pilgrims totalling about 700. A striking feature was the large proportion of young people numbering about 300. Almost all of whom would be seen pushing or taking turns to push an elderly or sick person in a wheelchair or stretcher bed. At Mass the Bishop calls for all volunteers to come forward to have their hands anointed as a sign of recognition and acknowledgement of the most noble work they do. The previous day the volunteers had made a 'guard of honour' around the sick and elderly in their group while their priests anointed them. In most areas the young people disappear as soon as they make the first Holy Communion (the cheekily captioned 'rite of exit') and so it was a marvel to behold to see Salford diocese with so many youths in their ranks.

Sr Generosa on Lourdes

We have come out of the evening Benediction in the underground Basilica and decide to sit outside the visitor centre near the Sanctuary of Our Lady as we watch pilgrims going and coming from the grotto. Sister Generosa begins to speak, reflectively, "*You see my brother, every parable in the Bible has an aspect of mercy. Lourdes is a holy place full of the dignity of mercy. You see and notice it immediately you arrive here. There is a kind of joy too in this, in arriving at this place.*

With the Immaculate Conception showing herself here it is poignant that the Holy Father Pope Francis chose the Feast of The Immaculate Conception to launch The Jubilee Year of Mercy." She wonders aloud if someone is able to pass on the message along the hierarchy of the Church to ask if it would be possible for The Holy Father to extend the Jubilee Year of Mercy by one more year? She says it is so important that everyone gets an opportunity to take the free offer of God's mercy that is available to all. She goes on. *"God is merciful. God is mercy. He is merciful towards all His people and all we need to do is to respond and take God's mercy by doing that which He commands us to do in the Scriptures"*.

She remembers particularly well our very first Mass soon after arrival, the Sunday Mass celebrated by a Cardinal in the Pope Pius X 25,000 seater underground Basilica. She goes on, *"The Epistle on Easter Vigil (Easter Saturday Mass) by Apostle Paul proclaims the Resurrection and marks the start of Eastertide. And Mary Magdalene remarking on Easter Sunday morning that 'they' had taken her Lord and she did not know where they had put him. The second Sunday is the Divine Mercy Sunday during which we all seek God's mercy with sincere hearts. The third Sunday would look at the breaking of the bread featuring the story of the two disciples on the road to Emmaus. Who ask each other after Jesus had gone,* **'Were not our hearts burning within us while he talked with us on the road and opened the Scriptures to us?'** *Luke 24:32. The fourth Sunday was The Good Shepherd Sunday, of the Shepherd who knows his flock and his flock which knows him. And the then practice of the shepherd walking in front of his flock with the flock following their shepherd. On the 5th Sunday highlighting the Love of God through the commandment of love in St John's Gospel. And the sixth Sunday where the promise is made that the Holy Spirit is to come at Pentecost as a witness to the Good News. We too are witnesses as people of faith and we are called upon to proclaim The Good News in Jerusalem, Judaea, Samaria all the way to the ends of the earth. (Acts 1: 1-11). On Pentecost Sunday The Holy Spirit comes as promised to lead and to strengthen us in our lives and in our faith as we preach the Good News. Finally* *comes Trinity Sunday at which the mystery of the three in one God is revealed."*

Wonderful. Back in the basilica due to its huge size we had followed the Mass taking place at the Altar quite some distance away via one of the many multi-screen CCTV screens posted within. At the trans-substantiation Sr and I looked at the close-up picture of the chalice on the giant screens and looked at each other. Clearly visible in the chalice was what appeared to us as...blood. Red as blood. Not wine anymore. We were kneeling during this time of Consecration. After Mass we discussed this between us. We had separately noticed this during Mass. His spilled blood for our sins.

At Offertory there came a long line of soldiers in regular army uniform but with no weapons, reverently bringing the Offertory gifts to the Cardinal who was leading the High Mass. We were to learn later that the same soldiers were part of the contingent that looks after and guards the Stations of The Cross up on the mountain. Providing friendly deterrence to mischief makers but mainly fulfilling the role of providing help and support if anyone faints or needs help as the mountain with The Stations is quite steep. If all the soldiers in the world were deployed to serve Christ, what other bother would there be in this world?

At the end of the torchlight procession each night in front of the Rosary Basilica everyone is given the Blessing by the procession leader after the concluding prayers. Everyone is then invited to offer the sign of peace to the people in their immediate vicinity. Sr told me one evening one of the people she gave the sign of peace to through a handshake said to her, *"Peace be with you too Sister. We will now meet in Heaven as we will not see each other again."* A simple but hugely profound message. Being from different continents the likelihood of our paths crossing again on this earth seemed practically nil. But what drew you and me to Lourdes during the same time period and for us to be standing next to each other at this particular procession is an act beyond our comprehension. In our everyday lives is it also not the case that we take the people we have for granted because we assume, they will still be around tomorrow? Do we not harbour grudges and unforgiveness as if we have control over the morrow? Perhaps I will never again be able to see that family member or neighbour whom I have refused to forgive or make peace with.

Sr continues her reflections about Lourdes. *"This is a peaceful place"*. Then she repeats herself very thoughtfully, as if meditating on the thought, or maybe in case I am not listening as I should. This place clearly has touched her heart. And it is not the last I hear of the peacefulness of Lourdes from her. As believers we give each other the sign of peace at Mass every day. Somehow it has an added meaning here on the grand Piazza with the Crowned Virgin Statue behind you and the Rosary Basilica right in front of you and all around you the huge sea of the deeply faithful who have journeyed with you on the evening procession.

I want to stay here
On the final day of our pilgrimage just as we are about to depart the next morning on Thursday, a lady in our pilgrimage group on her first visit to Lourdes remarks nostalgically, "I do not want to leave, I just want to stay here!" (Cf St Peter's at The Transfiguration, "Lord it is good

88

to be here!" Mt17:4). I do not blame her. I feel the same myself. I could also stay here all year round myself.

Another also says, "I do not want to leave…"
On our final night at dinner one lady is withdrawn and looks sad. I ask her, "Why are you looking so sad and sleepy?" 'I am not sleepy', she replies, 'Right now after this wonderful experience I am just thinking of all the issues and things awaiting me when I get back home.'

These sentiments of these two pilgrims in a way represent some of the more difficult parts of the pilgrimage "journey". The pre-travel phase, the journey from home to destination, the stay at the Shrine and all the activities, the prayers and the occasional purchase in the shops perhaps represent the "easy" parts of the "journey". The difficult part is living the journey of your life afterwards to show others you have been on pilgrimage. To be true to the numerous commitments you made to Our Lady at the Grotto and during your time here. To be true to the promises and undertakings you made in your written petitions that you generously left at each location where it was possible to do so. To be true to the quiet repentance and prayers for those that do not like you, openly or otherwise. To be true to the enthusiastic signs of peace you shared with strangers at each Mass and at the end of each Torchlight Procession, which you truly meant from the bottom of your heart but which sadly you fear you will find it difficult to extend to those closest to you. To be true to the promise to Our Lord Jesus never to sin again ("…*go and from now on, sin no more..*"**Jn8:11**):   All these acts of goodwill you are now obliged to extend to and share with your nearest and dearest back home. This often proves difficult and may be fraught with all sorts of pitfalls. And yet often it is the very reason why we have come on pilgrimage to seek Our Lady's intercession to rebuild bridges back to The Lord.

Lost her passport and cash on pilgrimage

A lady on her first pilgrimage to Lourdes in our group lost her wallet with personal belongings including passport, bank cards and all her cash while we were on our way to Lourdes by coach. She only discovered these were missing on arrival at Lourdes and searched everywhere on the coach and in her luggage but found nothing. Later she thought she might have forgotten these at the final services we stopped at. Luckily, after about 4 days a pilgrim in our group found a purchase receipt from these same services and their telephone number was used to confirm they had in fact seen and were keeping the wallet in question. Phewww!! Our pilgrimage organiser drove back all the way (the round journey taking a whole day) to this place to collect the missing package. It was the day of the final Mass that we were attending at Lourdes and the lady was to tell me later as her wallet had not arrived, she quietly said at Offertory time, *"Lord I have no money left and if you had wanted me to make an offertory you would have enabled my wallet to be here by now."* As she finished this silent contemplation the pilgrimage coordinator gently tapped her on the shoulder to deliver her passport and wallet. With everything intact. Providential coincidence. Miracles do still happen in our time, and in her ecstasy the lady simply drew out a wad of notes and threw them into the passing collection basket.

Another also lost her wallet and bank cards
Another lady in our pilgrimage group also told us that two days before travel she had had her wallet stolen which contained all her bank cards and some personal details. The saving grace was that her travel money had been safely left at home. She was not going to cancel her pilgrimage because of this and here she was with us.

Car accident just before travel
Another man also in our group had had a minor car accident a few days before travel. As he was not hurt he continued with his arrangements and made the pilgrimage.

Travel insurance
A man fell ill during our pilgrimage and was hospitalised. When we left he had not yet been discharged so he remained in hospital in Lourdes. His acquaintances told us that he had been reluctant to purchase travel insurance and had only done so at the very last minute. This insurance saved him a potentially huge medical bill in a foreign country.

I first came here 13 years ago
"13 years ago is when I first went to Lourdes and I was not even Catholic. My wife made me go! While standing at the Grotto with my back to it I felt a hand 'touch' me and turn my head to look behind me. I was standing out in the open area near the Grotto away from people. I do not know who touched me and there was no one in my immediate vicinity who could have touched me. Afterwards at Mass in Church a priest came to me and said, "*Can I give you a blessing?*" I said yes. I became a Catholic after that. I have not stopped coming to Lourdes since." In fact this man has become the

annual local pilgrimage organiser to Lourdes at his parish. His wife told me: "As a young girl I always wanted to come to Lourdes. I used to pray to get the opportunity. One day my aunt said, "Would you like to come to Lourdes?" I said yes. My prayer had been answered, and here I am now coming to Lourdes year after year. And with thanks to the Lord, now I come with my husband who is now arranging these pilgrimages for our parish every year." This man sadly passed away at the end of 2019. RIP.

My own healing

I too have a personal testimony of the power of God. Though not directly related to Lourdes. It happened on Friday 20th February 2015. While attending an all-night prayer meeting at the home of one of our small Christian community families my regular nose bleed recurred, which I had suffered in the previous two weeks. I had always suffered nose bleeds for about two weeks twice each year: at the start of the cold season in October and November and then as winter ends with the start of the warm season from about February to April. This bleeding would start sometimes when I sat at my desk at work, at home having a meal, chatting with friends, asleep in bed at night or during prayer in Church. Anywhere. And from my youth growing up I had always had nose bleed troubles during certain times of the year.

On this occasion while the Catholic priest leading our evening prayer session was preaching it just started, without warning as it always did. I quickly pulled out a wad of tissues from my shirt pocket to stem the bleeding. Noticing this the priest stopped preaching and asked me to follow him outside. He invited me to pray with him while he laid his hands on my head. He asked me if I believed that God was about to heal me. I replied with some doubt that yes He could. He laughed a little and asked me again if I really believed. I replied that I did. He asked boldly that in God's name this bleeding should stop immediately and never to come back again. He asked me to pray and believe. We prayed together. As he concluded the prayer and delivered The Lord's blessing to me I noticed that the bleeding just stopped. I never again had to use the huge quantity of tissues I was carrying around that night. To this day I HAVE NOT ENCOUNTERED ANY NOSE BLEEDING AGAIN. And I still believe. Glory be to God.

The Lord has done so much for us (including a cure)
An elderly pilgrim tells me, "Coming to Lourdes makes us see how lucky and blessed we are for all the things we take for granted in our lives. One day I was sitting in Lourdes and started speaking to a young girl. She responded in a very enthusiastic way and we had a really good chat. The child's mother was very surprised that she actually spoke so much. The common bond we derive from being members of the Catholic Church makes us able to express ourselves with openness and friendliness. I hope the young girl kept a more friendly attitude after that towards her family." He went on.

"Last night as my wife and I strolled around the hotel a group of 16 or 17-year olds greeted and spoke to us. They did not have to do this but they did. Perhaps they might not have done so elsewhere but because we were in a setting like Lourdes they felt able to do so. But they will also have done this because they must be well brought up Catholic children with good manners and behaviour. Two of these young people said they would be going to Edinburgh for University and I decided to do something for them for their kindness. I described the cafe owned by my sister in Edinburgh where they should go and ask for a free meal that I will make sure my sister grants them. It will be on me, bless these youngsters!

"And the other day at Mass I observed that people with hearing difficulties were given the chance to give a bidding prayer and this epitomises for me what Lourdes is all about. That was just fantastic!" His wife continues, "I was Church of England when I met my husband who was Catholic. At the time he worked 7 days a week and so I took the children to the Catholic Church every Sunday. I only became Catholic when our daughter was 15 but I did take them to Church every Sunday. I have now been to Lourdes 9 times. I come here to thank the Lord. I had back problems which got completely healed after coming here. The doctor certified that I needed no further treatment. I have not stopped thanking the Lord ever since."

The young wonderful angels
A pilgrim shares the following testimony: "*The young people from Salford, Manchester who did such wonderful volunteering bringing and looking after the sick and elderly in wheelchairs did it for me this time at Lourdes. Each time I saw the group from Salford I had a lump in my throat and tears in my eyes. To see such young people who are so well behaved, so hardworking and in such large numbers, so prayerfully too was so amazing. Such faith. To be so caring for the sick and elderly, their singing, the lap of honour for the whole congregation at that final and farewell Mass by the Salford group was just*

incredible." Her husband tells me, "*This is my 4ᵗʰ time coming to Lourdes. The most extraordinary things were the young people from Salford, who were kind, well behaved, had a choir out of this world and had everything so well organised. To have so many youths when it is no longer possible in many of our parishes is just great*". The husband tells me that today, as we leave Lourdes, is also the anniversary of the loss of their daughter some time ago and she would have been 44 today.

I have been coming here for 32 years

Another pilgrim says, "*I have been coming to Lourdes for the past 32 years. At first I did not even consider coming here, I just was not interested. Till I started and then never stopped! It has become a part of my DNA. Two other friends of mine have been coming here with me since 1997. I work in a hospice back in England and consider it very important that I am able to bring the prayer intentions of the people in the hospice who are themselves unable to come here. I must admit I have become hooked on Lourdes myself*".

I have been coming here since 1954 and only ever missed 1 year

Another pilgrim tells me she has been coming to Lourdes since 1954 (and this is 2018) and she only ever missed one year as her pilgrimage would have been too close to the birth of her son. Being a nurse she always came in the company of others sick or would simply come to spend her time attached to one of the hospitals doing charity work.

We have been to other pilgrimage sites too

Another says: "*My wife and I have been here 3 and 4 times respectively. We have been to other places too such as Padua,*

Medjugorje etc but somehow seem to have got hooked on Lourdes. We belong to the Legion of Mary back home. Since coming to Lourdes I have found peace in my life. I am not worried by anything. If a problem arises in my life I commend it to Our Lady who resolves them. And it works out fine every time. Lourdes is good for those whose faith has gone weak or even lapsed Catholics."

I come as a volunteer

"I have been coming to Lourdes for many years as a nurse helper. I volunteer when I am on leave from my day job in England. In that role you look after the sick in hospitals in Lourdes and you may only sometimes be seen when you bring the sick to the Procession, to Mass or to the Baths. Together with others you work shift patterns. For the sick to be brought here some elaborate planning and processes have to be followed. The trip has to be certified by the doctor before the sick person can travel to Lourdes. The more serious can still come to Lourdes and these usually need to be referred to St John's Ambulance who have the planes and capability to move such sick pilgrims. Within the hospitals at Lourdes there is a lot of work going on behind the scenes with large numbers of doctors, nurses, volunteers, priests and Sisters working with those committed to those hospitals. Even those very serious cases can still have arrangements made for them to join the Procession, Mass at the Grotto etc and will usually be brought with their breathing apparatuses, oxygen etc."

Many of the people who come to Lourdes seem to be repeat visits, comprising those who have been there before and as some pilgrims repeatedly mentioned, *"hooked to come back."*

The story of a musician

*"The musicians group with which played at Lourdes is a
Diocesan pilgrimage group that specifically meets in advance of
pilgrimages to Lourdes."* This man plays the organ or piano
and is comfortable with all types of organs available in
England. For him the benefit from doing this voluntary
work is what music means to the people who use it as an
accompaniment to prayer when they are at Lourdes. He
told me that it is very important to him as a person that
people would give him feedback on his music and how it
helps them to pray so he could understand how the
congregation empathised with him because you play the
instrument in a separate cubicle from the rest of the
congregation. He had been coming to Lourdes since 2001.
At a personal level for him, *"Lourdes recharges my batteries"*.
He said one year he came as a volunteer helping the sick
and elderly.

He had some ideas about embracing the young people.
*"The young can be harnessed by doing things that excite them
in the Church. By appreciating and encouraging them, giving
them space at the Shrine to relax and have a good time. But it
also involved providing the leadership to ensure they do not go
overboard. Music is my way of preaching the Good News of
The Gospel"*. And he wants to do more. He feels inspired by
what the doctors do. As an example he noted that the
Salford choir conductor is a medical doctor and a mother
who had just had a baby but had not taken time off to
nurse her baby. And she also came to Lourdes as a
volunteer doctor to help. He continues, *"I once spoke to her
back in England and she had said about her normal job that
sometimes she has just 'two hours sleep'"*. The musician was
also quite inspired by the cyclists from his Diocese who

cycled over 700 miles from North West England to Lourdes in just 10 days raising funds for the needy at Lourdes. He was inspired too by all those people who had been given various long service awards for their volunteering in services to the Church during this pilgrimage.

I could not say this in the presence of many people
"I could not say this before in the presence of many people. But earlier this week during Mass at the Grotto as I sit on the bench I hear a sensation as if the bench I am sitting on is vibrating or shaking from people deliberately playing with it. I need to go to the toilet as for many years I have been having bladder problems and my doctors have not been successful in treating my condition. At the toilets a distinctive bluish stone is passed out with the urine. Hours and days of pain seem to have been instantly relieved. The painful sensation that used to bother me so much has just gone, and I have not experienced the agony of what was now my lifetime condition in the past two days since that time during the Mass at the Grotto."

I first came here 60 years ago
Our group went to Lake Lourdes one afternoon and found there were already other pilgrims there swimming, some just relaxing their feet in the water, using paddle boats etc. Moments of relaxation like this are a useful integral part of a pilgrimage: recharging one's batteries midway through a pilgrimage. The young play games together. In conversation as we sat by the water one pilgrim told me of two couples from their Diocese who met at Lourdes and went on to get married. A friend and myself then chatted to a wheelchair bound pilgrim who first came to Lourdes about 60 years ago and had come on pilgrimage from time to time since

then. This time she came with her daughter and two grandchildren. The young children clearly dot on their nan whom they hug and play with. Happy families! Nan told us that in her local community a large part of her life is taken up helping others, including many asylum seekers and others in desperate situations. Once when asked how she made herself happy she responded, "*I find joy when I make others happy rather than focussing on self. Doing things for others is the best way I find happiness for myself*" Pope Francis would be proud to have her in his parish.

Are you Catholic?
Another pilgrim tells me over dinner, "A friend of mine and her husband had given me a lift in their car when we were involved in a minor accident with another car. When the other driver wanted to exchange contact details for insurance purposes, they asked if the driver of our car was Catholic. They were not but I said I was and the other car owner asked for both the driver's details as well as my own, saying that a fellow Catholic would not lie to them. A lovely testimony of the strong spiritual bond between members of the Catholic faith.

10   CONCLUDING REMARKS

Towards the end of William Shakespeare's famous play Macbeth, Macbeth himself soliloquises "*Life's but a walking shadow, a poor player that struts and frets his hour upon the stage and then is heard no more*". His wife Lady Macbeth had just killed herself. Lady Macbeth had been a powerful and dominant figure in both her household and the political arena, the so-called power behind the throne. Macbeth had now come to the realisation that even with the might and all the trappings of power and materiality in this world life could still be meaningless. In contrast Bernadette was a frail, quiet and shy girl who avoided all publicity and the worldly comforts. At one point in answer to a question she had said, *"The spring is not for me,"* when pressed on why she did not go to dip herself in the spring to rid herself of her own illnesses. Yet it is little Bernadette who did not depart this world to be heard of no more. Rather through her, more than 6 million pilgrims now go to Lourdes each year. Many come expecting to be healed. To be saved. To seek God. Because this is the very heart of God's mercy.

While on pilgrimage we will have remembered and prayed for those whom we left behind. Our disposition on return can play an important positive role in evangelising to those we left back home. The impact of a pilgrimage will differ from pilgrim to pilgrim, with some witnessing immediate renewal, and others not so, but in the end our God who speaks always answers all our prayers in His own time. Our pilgrimage will be complete when we are eventually found worthy of *"happiness in the other world"*. This must be the fundamental objective of our pilgrimage: marching towards the promised land of salvation which is full of freedom through experiencing Jesus Christ who rose to Heaven from the land of Jerusalem to open the way for us towards The Father. Every pilgrim could learn from the anonymous pilgrim: *"By the grace of God I am a human person and a Christian; by my actions, a great sinner; by my condition a pilgrim without a roof, being of the lowliest species that goes wandering from place to place. My possessions are a sack on my shoulders with a bit of dry bread and a Holy Bible that I carry under my clothing. No other thing do I have."* - **The Way of a**

Pilgrim **(R. M. French (translator)).** I too am lowly, no more than the anonymous pilgrim and my faith gifted to me by my parents is my only gift to you.

At the end of your pilgrimage it would be fair to ask: "*What did you want to change or achieve when you set out to come on pilgrimage? What was your definite purpose for coming?*" Well, when you return home, it is not enough to just look at the photos and videos and share these with friends and family and then close this chapter of your life. You have to make the pilgrimage a living and continuing journey of your life. The Holy Father Pope Francis on returning from the World Youth Day in Rio in 2013 said he wanted the post-Youth Day Rio to be a mess. Like a field hospital after a battle. And he also wanted the Church to be like that. For the field hospital is where the injured and the weary come to have their wounds attended to and lives saved, where they come to have temporary rest so they can resume their journey towards safety and peace. When you depart Lourdes, you too must consider the Holy Sanctuary to be the field hospital of Our Lord Jesus Christ together with His Mother Our Lady. Where we all come and return to be healed of our ills both physical and spiritual. And as we go away to exhort in unison, "***Stay with us Lord, stay with us Lord, stay with us on our journey***." May your wandering from place to place on your earthly journey lead you in the direction of the field hospital of our Lord Jesus Christ and his Mother, Our lady of Lourdes with the faith and humility of the anonymous pilgrim. For therein truly lies THE HEART OF GOD'S MERCY. Amen.

ANNEX 1   WHY SHOULD WE GO ON PILGRIMAGE?

Why do people go on pilgrimages, or more specifically why should you and I go on this pilgrimage? Because simply we are all sinners and therefore need God's mercy. *"Why do you call me good?"* Jesus answered. *"No one is good--except God alone* (Mark10:18). In the 2015 "***Apostolic Exhortation Evangelii Gaudium (The joy of the Gospel) The Holy Father Pope Francis*** writes "*There are Christians whose lives seem like Lent without Easter...*". © Libreria Editrice Vaticana. (Used with permission.) And in Lamentations 3: 17, 21-23, 26, "*My soul is bereft of peace. I have forgotten what happiness is...But this I call to mind, and therefore I have hope: the steadfast love of the Lord never ceases, His mercies never come to an end; they are new every morning. Great is your faithfulness...It is good that one should wait quietly for the salvation of the Lord*". God's mercy can bring us the Easter, the peace, the joy that we seek in the Lord.

Today many of us are damaged, sometimes repeatedly, by fragile or broken relationships in the home, in the workplace and society as a whole. We hold on to old hurts and scars from the past that we are unable to let go in order to move on. We suffer from a lack of spiritual healing for our sins or transgressions which we have not been able or are unwilling to confess to receive absolution through the Sacrament of Reconciliation. We keep these hurts bottled up inside. Persuading us away from sin and demonstrating the enormity of sinning St Alphonsus starkly warns, "*What punishment would that subject deserve who, while his king was giving him a command, contemptuously turned his back upon him to go and transgress his orders?*"

In addition to sin we also lack a physical healing such as from disease, injury to the body or infirmity. Some diseases that afflict us are due to us not having spiritual healing. For these we need God's mercy for He is The Healer. The Master. The Almighty. Often we suffer from a lack of forgiveness which we then disguise as the controversial "*forgive but not forget*". Either one forgives or does not forgive: when you forgive you forget, obviously without having to be naïve about it. In reality we very often simply cannot bring ourselves to be forgiving. For true forgiveness is unconditional. "*Then Peter came to Jesus and asked, "Lord, how many times shall I forgive my brother who sins against me? Up to seven times?"* Jesus answered, *"I tell you, not just seven times, but seventy-seven times!"* (Matthew 18 v 21-22). Jesus did not place a condition or a limit on forgiveness. Unconditional forgiveness. Which is why perhaps the Holy Father Pope Francis in His wisdom declared the 2016 Liturgical year the Jubilee Year of Mercy in order to help mankind receive and reflect on mercy. Perhaps the Jubilee Year of Mercy should have been extended to more than one year? My personal view is that with forgiveness and mercy the world would be a totally different place than it is or will ever be. People come to Lourdes for many different reasons: the sick and infirm, those who seek inner peace through the Sacraments in particular that of Reconciliation. What better place for all of these than Lourdes: The heart of God's mercy.

At one of our community Masses the lay leaders once asked the priests to make some special prayers for the sick and elderly in the community. At the final blessing the priests asked anyone who was elderly or had an ailment physical or spiritual to come forward to kneel before the Altar for some prayers, anointing and asperging with Holy water and the blessing. Did the priests misjudge their congregation for EVERYONE, young and old came forward to be prayed for and receive anointing oils and to be sprinkled with Holy Water! Every one of us is wounded in one way or another and needs healing. Every one of us. Some physical ailments are an expression of the wounding that has taken place on the inside. Lourdes is a good place to start. Our Lady went there to prepare a way for us back to the Lord, and reached out to us through Bernadette. Our Lady already knew that we are sinners and it hurt her to see the world heading away from God's mercy. So she came to Lourdes, to establish the heart of God's mercy so that sinners would be forgiven through *"Penance, Penance, Penance"*.

A pilgrimage is the tent of a personal and intimate meeting between God Himself and you (and me). It should take the form of a journey to enter the tent of a meeting with Mary, the Mother of our Lord Jesus Christ. She is our intercessor. A pilgrimage tends to take the form of both a physical and a spiritual journey but can also take the spiritual form only. But if it only takes the physical form without spirituality or the spiritual component, then it is NOT a pilgrimage. It would have been reduced to being a mere social trip, a tour, a tourism adventure, a mere visit. *"Go and tell the priests...to bring the people here in procession."* in one of the messages Our Lady gave to St Bernadette encouraging us to return to God through prayerful processions - journeys in pilgrimage.

Lost in the drudgery of our daily realities and anxieties, we need to discover and rediscover ourselves through reflection, meditation, prayer, examination of our consciences, often in silence or via new experiences that can usually be lived through a pilgrimage. We can do this through retracing the footsteps of The Lord, encounters with Our Lady, or prayerfully experiencing places graced by some of the great Saints in the Church's history. The bigger Marian shrines like Lourdes and Fatima and the smaller ones can be privileged places for a meeting with her and her Son. The womb of Our Lady was the first Shrine, the tent of a meeting between divinity and humanity on which the Holy Spirit descended and which *"the power of the Most High with its shadow"* Lk1:35 made possible the birth of Christ. Through Our Lady, the final destination and purpose of a pilgrimage is meeting with and resting on the bosom of The Lord Jesus Christ Himself.

ANNEX 2   WHEN DOES A PILGRIMAGE START AND END?

So you are preparing to go to Lourdes on pilgrimage? When therefore does your pilgrimage start? Does it start on the day you board the plane, coach, train or bus to the holy place? Does it commence when you touch down on arrival? Does it start when you get into Church for your first prayers or celebration of the Holy Mass? Does it start when you start to go around with your pilgrimage guide explaining all those things which will satisfy your curiosities and answer all those questions in a manner that you feel it was all a worthwhile financial investment to save for? And for which you denied yourself expensive treats so you could come to this once-in-a-lifetime destination? Does it start when you begin to feel contended that it was a 'win-win' social and emotional outing that did not disappoint? Or when you have gone to Confession at the Sanctuary and feel you have now been 'purified'?

No. In fact your pilgrimage should start at the moment you make the decision to go to the holy places. It may have been last year, the year before that, six months ago, or whenever you effectively made that decision. And your whole being should begin to change from that moment on. Irreversibly. For the greater glory. For that is when your pilgrimage begins. And when does it end?

Well, once started a pilgrimage should really never end. Going on a pilgrimage must be a beginning (a new beginning), the lighting up of a candle, a fire in your heart, the kick-starting of a never-ending new spirituality within oneself. This is because our whole lives must henceforth become a continuous pilgrimage, a sacred journey, drawing daily inspiration from what St Paul says to the Philippians "...*forgetting what is behind and straining toward what is ahead...*". Phil3:13. Hence the act of visiting the Holy Places becomes the salt, the lubricant, the re-charge station of our faith. The new beginning. Repeat visits to Pilgrimage Shrines or sites become the renewal milestones of one's covenant with Christ Jesus, each one preferably a higher milestone than the previous ones. I hope these principles will guide your life-- as they should mine too.

ANNEX 3   SOME USEFUL PRAYERFUL ACTIVITIES AND PERSONAL ACTIONS DURING PILGRIMAGE

Activities

1. Visit the Reconciliation Chapel for Confession/Penance at the start, and as often as is needed during a pilgrimage—we are all sinners;
2. It is ideal to go to Mass each day, there are quite a number held at different times and at different locations. Some additional ones are arranged by visiting pilgrimage groups;
3. Do try to pray the Rosary each day--there are several communal Rosary sessions each day at the Grotto and at the Baths;
4. Every night at 9 p.m. there is The Torchlight Rosary Procession that starts from and ends with the blessing in front of the Rosary Basilica on the piazza;
5. Do visit the Holy Grotto often, even if only to sit quietly in prayer, meditation or quiet conversation with Our Lady and/or her Son;
6. Make an effort to visit the Adoration Chapel for the Exposition of The Blessed Sacrament. Open to all each day all day for Adoration;
7. If possible, try to go and wash at the Baths at least once during pilgrimage;
8. If possible, try to go to the underground Basilica for Benediction with The Blessed Sacrament each day at 5pm; there are also healing services on some days as well as International Masses on Sundays and Wednesday at 9.30 a.m;
9. Try not to not leave Lourdes without doing The

Stations of The Cross. There are the High Stations on the mountain and Low Stations on flat low terrain for those who may have mobility difficulties. The Stations of the Cross afford you the opportunity to suffer with and for Christ, as we all should from time to time;

10. As the last act of the day each day, place yourself in God's hands, and then peacefully drift off to sleep…

11. Of course, there are numerous other activities that groups or individuals can do while on pilgrimage.

Personal actions/reflections (*as you suffer with and for Christ*)

a) Commend yourself and your day's activities totally to God at the start of each day;

b) Always admit that you are a sinner (*"…perhaps I have not suffered enough…"--St Bernadette)*;

c) Speak to God with all your heart (*"…speak to God as if you were alone with Him, familiarly and with confidence and love, as to the dearest and most loving of friends. "--St Alphonsus Liguori)*;

d) Let go: Do let go of all the bitterness, grudges, hatred, difficult or vengeful thoughts, ill will towards those who hurt you at some stage. Forgive those that usually come to your mind when you see or think of those who have hurt or disappointed you. **And let go for good**;

e) Forgive everyone, in particular those that have declared that they will never forgive you;

f) Pray for those who are close to you, especially those in the habit of repeatedly and/or wilfully hurting you;

g) Place yourself in God's care *"Offer yourself to God*

that He may do with you what He pleases."--St Alphonsus Liguori;

h) If at all possible, do not hurry your visits to the holy sites or your activities during pilgrimage…take your time… it adds immensely to the prayerfulness of everything you do. Keep reminding yourself that a pilgrimage is totally different from a tourism visit.

Many of the suggested actions are to do with mercy and forgiveness, perhaps the two most difficult issues in the world today.

ANNEX 4   SOME PRAYERS FOR YOU AND ME

Pope Francis has composed a special prayer for the Jubilee Year of Mercy which ran from 8 December 2015 to 20 November 2016. In the prayer, the Holy Father entreats the Lord to make the Jubilee of Mercy a year of grace so that the Church, "*with renewed enthusiasm, may bring good news to the poor, proclaim liberty to captives and the oppressed, and restore sight to the blind.*"

Pope Francis' prayer for the Jubilee year of Mercy
Lord Jesus Christ,
you have taught us to be merciful like the heavenly Father,
and have told us that whoever sees you sees Him.
Show us your face and we will be saved.
Your loving gaze freed Zacchaeus and Matthew from being enslaved by money;
the adulteress and Magdalene from seeking happiness only in created things;

made Peter weep after his betrayal,
and assured Paradise to the repentant thief.
Let us hear, as if addressed to each one of us, the words that
you spoke to the Samaritan woman:
"If you knew the gift of God!"
You are the visible face of the invisible Father,
of the God who manifests his power above all by
forgiveness and mercy:
let the Church be your visible face in the world, its Lord
risen and glorified.
You willed that your ministers would also be clothed in
weakness
in order that they may feel compassion for those in
ignorance and error:
let everyone who approaches them feel sought after, loved,
and forgiven by God.

Send your Spirit and consecrate every one of us with its anointing,
so that the Jubilee of Mercy may be a year of grace from the Lord,
and your Church, with renewed enthusiasm, may bring good news to the poor,
proclaim liberty to captives and the oppressed,
and restore sight to the blind.
We ask this through the intercession of Mary, Mother of Mercy,
you who live and reign with the Father and the Holy Spirit forever and ever.

Amen.
© Libreria Editrice Vaticana. Used with permission

Prayer to St Bernadette
St Bernadette – Teach us to serve and pray
In Lourdes You experienced the joys and trials of family life
You saw Mary eighteen times at the rock
You called the sinners to penance
The priests to edify the Church of God
The pilgrims to come in procession
You reported the name of Mary, the Immaculate Conception
You desired ardently to receive the Body of the Lord, and to live of it
You knew shame and suspicion, mockery and humiliation
You bore witness to what you saw and believed with such determination
You answered the call of the Lord.

With you Bernadette, WE go to the Grotto, to contemplate Mary, full of grace, to hear her say 'Do whatever he tells you'.

With you Bernadette, WE reply I promise, I will. Saint Bernadette teach us to receive the good news.

With you Bernadette, WE wish to hear the call of penance, to walk in the path of conversion, to live in humility

With you Bernadette, WE take up our Cross, we say 'Holy Mary, Mother of God, pray for us sinners

With you Bernadette, WE go and wash at the springs of mercy

With you Bernadette, WE say Yes to the will of God, by becoming servants of the little ones, the poor and the sick

With you Bernadette, WE look on the other as a person, Saint Bernadette, teach us to love and to serve

With you Bernadette, WE go to meet the Lord in the Eucharist. WE go to drink at the Spring of the Living Water of the Word of God. WE go in procession, together as a Church in the footsteps of Christ.

With you Bernadette, WE shall go and repeat the Name of the Lady to the World, 'I am the Immaculate Conception'.

Saint Bernadette, teach us to pray to Mary each day, Mother of God and our Mother: 'Hail Mary, full of Grace'.

O Mary conceived without sin, pray for us who have recourse to you
Our Lady of Lourdes, Pray for us. Saint Bernadette Pray for us.

Amen
Used with permission. Direct from Lourdes Catholic Gift Shop

Prayer to Our Lady of Lourdes:
O ever immaculate Virgin, Mother of mercy, health of the
sick, refuge of sinners, comfort of the afflicted, you know
my wants, my troubles, my sufferings; deign to cast upon
me a look of mercy. By appearing in the Grotto of Lourdes,
you were pleased to make it a privileged sanctuary, whence
you dispense your favours, and already many sufferers have
obtained the cure of their infirmities both spiritual and
corporal, I come, therefore, with unbounded confidence, to
implore your material intercession. Obtain, O loving
Mother, the grant of my requests. I will endeavour to
imitate your virtues, that I may one day share your glory,
and bless you in eternity.
Amen.

Our Lady of Lourdes, pray for us;
St Bernadette, pray for us; Amen.

My prayer to Bernadette
"Bernadette I would like to be like you;
Obedient little girl you listened to Aquero;
Teach all young hearts to be prayerful like you;
And all parents to grow their children with faith like yours;
Praying the Rosary as you always;
That our names be written in the Book of Life in the
Heavens above;
Teach us to accept the life of sufferings with unparalleled
grace;
To have Jesus alone for master;
And like you at the appointed time to die a holy death;

To rest forever only on the bosom of the Lord. Amen."

© **Joseph Foroma**
2021

HAIL MARY
"Hail Mary, full of grace. The Lord is with thee. Blessed art thou among women, and blessed is the fruit of thy womb, Jesus.
"Holy Mary, Mother of God, pray for us sinners, now and at the hour of our death. Amen."

GLORY BE TO GOD
"Glory be to the Father, and to the Son, and to the Holy Spirit: As it was in the beginning, is now, and ever shall be, world without end. Amen."

"In the Name of the Father, and of the Son and of the Holy Spirit. Amen."

RFFERENCES
EUCHARISTIC CELEBRATION ON THE OCCASION OF THE 150th ANNIVERSARY OF THE APPARITIONS OF THE BLESSED VIRGIN MARY HOMILY OF HIS HOLINESS BENEDICT XVI, Prairie, Lourdes, Sunday, 14 September 2008 © Copyright 2008 - Libreria Editrice Vaticana: diritti.lev@spc.va

Franciscan Media publications, www.franciscanmedia.org

MSM Publications, In Lourdes 1844 Bernadette Nevers 1879; https://www.msm-editions.fr/

Direct from Lourdes website: www.DirectFromLourdes.com;

The Lourdes Sanctuary; website: https://www.lourdes-france.org/en/
With the kind permission of Sanctuaire ND de Lourdes, Pôle Communication

Narrations of the tour guides on my various pilgrimages to Lourdes

Testimonies from fellow pilgrims.

Author of: *Reflections on Bishop Xaverio Johnsai Munyongani: When God called ... his job here was done.* 2021.

Published by DanTs Media Publishing

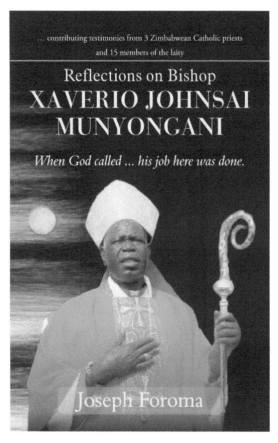

Available on major online book distributing outlets.